TRANSFORMING FATE INTO DESTINY

Hay House Titles of Related Interest

TRANSFORMING FATE INTO DESTINY

A New Dialogue with Your Soul

ROBERT OHOTTO

HAY HOUSE, INC.
Carlsbad, California • New York City
London • Sydney • Johannesburg
Vancouver • Hong Kong • New Delhi

Published and distributed in the United States by: Hay House, Inc.: www.hayhouse.com • ***Published and distributed in Australia by:*** Hay House Australia Pty. Ltd.: www.hayhouse.com.au • ***Published and distributed in the United Kingdom by:*** Hay House UK, Ltd.: www.hayhouse.co.uk • ***Published and distributed in the Republic of South Africa by:*** Hay House SA (Pty), Ltd.: www.hayhouse.co.za • ***Distributed in Canada by:*** Raincoast: www.raincoast.com • ***Published in India by:*** Hay House Publishers India: www.hayhouse.co.in

Design: Tricia Breidenthal

The author of this book does not dispense medical advice or prescribe the use of any technique as a form of treatment for physical, emotional, or medical problems without the advice of a physician, either directly or indirectly. The intent of the author is only to offer information of a general nature to help you in your quest for emotional and spiritual well-being. In the event you use any of the information in this book for yourself, which is your constitutional right, the author and the publisher assume no responsibility for your actions.

Please note that the names of clients and family members in this book have been changed, and various other details of their stories have been altered to protect their privacy.

Library of Congress Cataloging-in-Publication Data

Ohotto, Robert.
Transforming fate into destiny : a new dialogue with your soul / Robert Ohotto. -- 1st ed.
p. cm.
ISBN 978-1-4019-1155-3 (tradepaper)
1. Fate and fatalism--Religious aspects. I. Title.

BL235.O36 2008
204'.4--dc22 2007033422

ISBN: 978-1-4019-1155-3

11 10 09 08 4 3 2 1
1st edition, March 2008

Printed in the United States of America

For Dad, Mom, and Jenny:

Your Fate has become my Destiny.

CONTENTS

FOREWORD

by Caroline Myss

The most life-transforming words a person can utter are: "For what reason have I been born?" Most people assume that in speaking those few words, they're asking a simple question. While it appears to be an ordinary query that usually arises at moments of frustration or during times of great introspection, the deeper truth is that this is a sacred invocation of the heavens in which the individual is asking to have the burden of Fate lifted so that the magnificence of his or her Destiny can begin to unfold. To be sure, such an unveiling of cosmic power requires that the person undergo one test after another, as Destiny isn't given to the uninitiated. Rather, the one who utters the question is unconsciously saying to God, "I'm ready to release the illusions that my ego has gathered around me for safety and let my soul serve the purpose for which it has incarnated."

For most people, of course, even thinking about the difference between the governing forces of Fate and Destiny sounds like the text of ancient Greek mythologies, and they're right. But so were the ancient Greeks who, in their trusting allegiance to the cosmic pantheon of gods and goddesses, recognized that human beings didn't stand upon this earth all by themselves. Something—some power greater than themselves—was influencing the events of their everyday lives. Everything was just too well coordinated and too filled with integrated systems of cause and effect to be held together by luck. No, a plan existed somewhere, but where?

A plan much greater than us that contains and coordinates all of life must exist off the earth, somewhere "out there." It must be above and around us, thought these ancient Greeks, written like a code in the heavens that surround us, as the cosmos is the dwelling place of the gods. The coordinates to the great code of these deities were so obvious—of course, the planets. The beings in the cosmos that had patterns independent of the stars seemed somehow to have an authority all their own and independent of each other, ruling over our Fate and Destiny. And so the ancient Greeks studied the heavens, noting that the planets seemed to embody characteristics unique to each one and oddly intimate to each human life. Somehow the vast abyss of the night sky and its sparkling display of stars, planets, comets, and cycles of the moon were woven into the fabric of each soul. To look up was to look within; to go within was to see God.

And so began Western culture's dialogue with the cosmic forces, which thousands of years ago first pondered the same question we continue to ask ourselves today: "For what reason have I been born?" And just like the ancient Greeks and Romans, the most accurate science in interpreting the nature of an individual's Fate and Destiny remains the study of the planets, which govern the great archetypal patterns of the galaxy. Astrology, which gave birth to astronomy in the later centuries of the Enlightenment, is among the first sciences of the soul.

I believe that we're destined to ask about our Fate—or fated to ask about our Destiny, if you will. That is to say, we can't avoid reaching the moment in our lives when we each, in our own way, seek out the greater meaning and purpose of our lives. It's as inevitable on the human journey as are the physical and biological stages of maturation that occur within the body automatically.

I've seen individuals struggle for many years in their quest to understand their Sacred Contracts with God, and long ago I recognized that Fate and Destiny are two forces locked within every Sacred Contract. One choice belongs to your ego and the other to your soul. The ego chooses out of fear, and thus whatever the person creates will lead to a fated outcome. But the soul follows interior guidance and creates through Divine instructions—that's how Destiny unfolds.

In a sense, each day of your life is suspended between the magnetic pull of Fate and Destiny, as there's never one grand and final choice that closes the book on your Fate and seals the good fortune of your Destiny forever. Every choice you make is an investment in either one or the other, each day of your life.

How much difference does knowing your Fate from your Destiny make? You may as well ask yourself, *Would a life created out of fear be different from one molded from courage and truth?* To live your Destiny means that you must refine your self-esteem and not compromise your honor and integrity. You must follow the unknown and wake up an optimist rather than a pessimist. Destiny isn't a reward; it's earned every day of your life, one choice at a time. How do you find this path? It's first discovered by becoming a congruent person. You must change before opportunities can expand, as you're the force that animates the events of your life.

We're now living in an age where the wisdom of the ancient mystery schools has once again resurfaced into the mainstream, knowledge once restricted to monasteries and underground organizations. Astrology was among this hidden sacred information—not because it was considered nonsense, but because it was recognized as among the most powerful sciences through which a person could unlock his or her interior mysteries, among them the secrets of Fate and Destiny. It was viewed as sacred and not just thought of as "information" because the astrologer and the recipient understood that upon learning the content of one's personal chart, a sacred work was being unlocked. The recipient was in fact being shown a personal cosmic text, a soul document, and was therefore obligated to act according to the revelations given during the reading. An astrological reading was a sacred event that was often conducted within a devotional atmosphere, so highly regarded was the field of grace around such an experience.

Although centuries have passed since those days of candlelit rituals and astrologer-priests, the potency of astrological readings and their power to unlock knowledge related to your Destiny remains no less real. Time has no bearing upon the governing forces of the planets, regardless of how scientific we have become. For in spite of our addiction to technology, still we can't stop ourselves from seeking answers to the same questions that drew the ancients to their astrologers, who wondered: *For what reason have I been born? What is my Destiny upon this earth?* And the tool these great masters of insight turned to then—as now—was astrology.

Based on his years of professional work as an intuitive and astrologer, Robert Ohotto has written a magnificent book on Fate and Destiny. In fact, he's written an absolutely captivating one. His understanding of these two forces as archetypes is superb, and his application of how they influence you will leave you thinking he wrote this book just for you. I've known Robert for years, and I've had the pleasure of teaching with him many times. He's not an average intuitive or astrologer; he's a scholar who knows the mythic roots of his work and not just the surface basics. The planets and their voices are in his cell tissue and speak through him as a guiding intuitive voice—a voice that he has made accessible for everyone through this book.

I've taught the subject of Fate and Destiny many times, and in reading this book, I discovered more about them—that's the finest compliment I can pay a colleague. To learn from another teacher about a subject that you've also taught is a tribute to the excellent work and research of that person. Well done, Robert. I have no doubt that your work as an intuitive and astrologer—including the writing of this book—is a part of your Destiny.

PREFACE

Becoming a Professional Intuitive: My Story

I'm often asked, "What exactly is it that you do, and how did you end up working as a professional intuitive?" Each time before answering, I have to grin as I think, *Do you really want to know?* Because some people undoubtedly expect a story of a near-death experience, engendering me with sudden psychic gifts of perception, or a story of "beings" appearing to me. While I've had some profound mystical experiences that have catalyzed my path (and yes, the occasional "being" encounter), they were—and are—few and far between. To be honest, the truth is much less dramatic.

My intuitive skills developed gradually, as did my life's purpose—no fireworks or visions here. As a child growing up in Colorado and Wisconsin, I was often remarkably insightful, although that often did me little good in my home as I negotiated life with two alcoholic parents, including an abusive father. At the same time, I was trying to fit into a culture that I felt didn't accept me for being an acutely sensitive young boy. Luckily, I developed into an excellent athlete during adolescence, which was my saving grace, as it gave me some confidence. In fact, it opened the door to my intuitive abilities in many regards, as intuition is the offspring of believing in oneself.

When I was 11, my parents enrolled me in a Tae Kwon Do class that not only gave me that confidence (as I won many trophies), but it also introduced me to the mind-body-spirit connection. More important, during the two years I practiced that martial art, I got my first taste of Zen, an inner space of clarity out of which intuitive perception is born. I remember going to tournaments and hanging out with the adults, who came to me for life and relationship advice. Word soon spread that I offered very helpful counsel, and I often found myself staying up late as I engaged in deep philosophical discussions with adults 15 years my senior! They remarked how insightful and perceptive I was for such a young man.

In high school, I excelled as an athlete in track-and-field, and that led to a scholarship to a small state university, which I rejected. Instead, I opted for a city-based liberal arts college in Minneapolis to fulfill ambitions of being a theater and psychology major. I yearned to explore the creative and sensitive aspects of my psyche. By the time I left for school, my parents were divorced (for the second time) and had both gone through drug and alcohol rehab.

As my parents began their new lives, I started mine. Like many other college freshmen, I struggled with my identity and the deeper meaning of my purpose. I no longer had athletics to support an empowered sense of my own confidence, and I felt myself sinking into a deeply depressed and confused state.

As the saying goes, "When the student is ready, the teacher appears." Mine came in the guise of a good friend named Ben, whom I'd met early in my freshman year. One night that following summer, he asked me if

I'd like to have a tarot card reading. Fascinated and willing to suspend belief—not to mention eager to know my future (who wouldn't be, right?)—I agreed to it. I was greatly intrigued when his insights into my life proved quite accurate. *How did he do it?* I wondered.

Ben could sense my interest and asked if I'd like to learn how to read the cards, too. I enthusiastically said that I would. That summer I spent countless hours with him studying my first intuitive tool. When properly understood, the tarot is really an esoteric Kabbalistic divination system. This was my initiation into a larger life path, as well as studies that brought about the reemergence and further development of my intuitive abilities—abilities that allow me to see beyond the surface of someone's personality.

As it turned out, Ben belonged to a metaphysical organization that had a very developed curriculum of Western esoteric studies such as the tarot, alchemy, Christian mysticism, and ancient Greek and Egyptian texts. A couple of years after learning about tarot with Ben, I was invited to join this group and began to make the transition from being Catholic, forged by the religious dogma of my childhood, to being an initiate on an esoteric spiritual path.

The very act of studying something changes you, and I was also profoundly transformed by putting this knowledge into action via sacred rituals, meditations, and creating artistic representations of the symbols. Oftentimes it was no joyride, especially as I began to heal my psyche through confronting the early wounding of my childhood environment.

After two years of diligent study, eventually the time came for me to learn how to cast an astrological birth chart, or "natal chart," which maps precisely where the planets were in relationship to the exact moment and geographical location of one's birth. I took to astrology right away and was able to use this tool to see deep into people with amazing accuracy. I soon discovered that I had a unique talent with the birth chart and could use it to quickly grasp the essence of the unfolding, timing, and purpose of someone's life. This tool also allowed me to enter right into their psychological patterning in ways that would take even the most adept therapist months—if not years—to accomplish. Consequently, I found myself increasingly looking outside of the clinical psychological model I was learning in college, more intrigued by the metaphysical study of the human psyche, otherwise known as alchemy and depth/Jungian psychology.

As my college years drew to a close, another dear friend, Cara, suggested that I begin doing intuitive and astrological work professionally. I'd conducted numerous readings for her and her family members, all with incredible accuracy in terms of charting their patterns and life purposes. Not resonating with further academic study of clinical psychology and having realized that my ambitions to be an actor lacked the right intention, I took her advice.

Although my professional life followed many twists and turns in those first few years, I never looked back. At points I did take breaks from working professionally in the intuitive arts. In fact, for a number of years I left the tool of astrology behind while I took some time to explore the Eastern spiritual and philosophical traditions such as yoga, Buddhism, Sufism, and Hinduism. Eventually, I returned professionally to the intuitive arts, but without using astrology. Instead, I just read clients through pure intuitive/psychic perception. In tandem with this, I began a career as a yoga instructor in Chicago.

Around this time, I was introduced to the brilliant work of renowned medical intuitive Caroline Myss. She taught me so much regarding the nature of perception and the human energy system. After spending some years learning from Caroline's work via her books and audio tapes, I got invited to sit in as a studio audience member for a series on medical intuition that she recorded in Chicago with Norman Shealy (a neurosurgeon who worked with her in developing her skills as a medical intuitive).

When Norm walked into the room, it was like seeing an old friend—somehow I *knew* him, and he had the same experience of recognition. He came up to me and asked, "What do you do? Who are you?" That led to us having dinner each night after the long days of recording in the studio. I disclosed to Norm that I was a budding intuitive, which he'd already sensed. He then invited me down to St. Louis to a five-day intensive training with him and Caroline.

Although I'd met Caroline at the studio in Chicago, we actually didn't speak much since she was completely focused on the recording. But once I got to St. Louis, I walked into the room and began teasing her, which luckily led to us becoming great friends. She has become much more than a friend to me; she has also been a huge mentor and teacher. Not a day goes by without my being grateful for her support and presence in my life.

Inspired by Caroline's work with intuition and health, I combined the various teachings I'd studied with insights I'd gained over the years regarding the human psyche and intuitive development. My skills then began to mature to a new level of specificity and application. The data that I received on each client allowed me to track the psychic inheritances from family and culture that often spanned generations.

As time went by, I sensed that I was entering into the soul of each client and realized I needed something to help me establish symbolic coordinates so that I could get my bearings and better interpret the soul's intention. (The soul speaks through the language of symbols.) It was then that I returned to my favorite symbolic tool, astrology, with newfound vision. This launched my practice to new heights and rekindled my passion for mythology, which led me into a deep study of the classics and archetypes and how they interact within the human psyche and shape our life purpose.

At this juncture, Caroline (seeing me as the brilliant intuitive and astrologer I was proving to be!) asked me to write articles for her Website newsletter and teach at her institute in Chicago. Before I knew it, I was being scouted by publishers and doing lecture tours around the country.

It's been 17 years since my friend Ben introduced me to this path. Now I work primarily as an intuitive astrologer, but to be honest, I've never been a big fan of labels. In my experience, most of them inevitably become limitations to the ever-expanding aspects of our nature. Furthermore, the way I use astrology has *nothing* to do with columns found in most glossy magazines. Yet I am an intuitive, teacher, writer, astrologer, TV and radio-show personality, and now—with this book—an author.

What Is a Professional Intuitive Reading?

So what do I *see* when I do a reading, and how does it work? First, these days the session is almost never in person, but is done over the phone. About an hour before an appointment, I go to work. I shift my focus and awareness down into my body, which grounds me in the present moment. Once my mind is settled, I take my awareness and enter into the psychic field of my client. When I've remotely connected with my client's psyche, soul, and energy, I begin to receive and write down my first intuitive impressions. I've trained myself to access this information in a structured way that I've developed over the years. This allows me to better organize the data so that it makes sense and begins to construct a picture of the person I'm working with. Slowly but surely, just as our eyes and brain process visual input from our environments, I begin to perceive various things about the person I'm going to call for the reading.

What is it that I see about my clients? Generally, there are a few things I intuitively perceive: their soul's intention in this lifetime, the patterning they've incarnated into through their family, the legacy each parent has passed down to them psychologically (I call this psychic DNA), how they've created their lives out of that, where they're losing power, what patterns are most animated, their current cycles of development, and what's trying to die and to be born for them. I often deepen my understanding by coordinating these impressions with their astrological birth charts.

The information I receive and perceive during a reading requires an immense amount of integration. We are, after all, highly complex beings. For the purposes of this book, I'm going to focus on one piece of the greater puzzle that connects to your journey on Earth. It's the piece that I feel is most needed in our current struggles to become who we were born to be. It animates our highest potential and fulfills our destiny both as individuals and collectively.

As you read this book, I'll teach you to assess crucial aspects of yourself and educate you regarding the ways in which you may be unconsciously violating your life's purpose and blocking yourself from your highest good. I feel that it's extremely important for all of us to understand this in order to embrace the crucial crossroads we're at collectively. A new dawning of consciousness is now birthing on the planet, and a different dominant global pattern is starting to manage creation here on Earth. If we're to gracefully transition to our next level of understanding, we need new tools and models of perception—and this is why, in part, I wrote this book for you.

After years of working with clients, I began to see that certain themes and patterns were consistently emerging. Often, I felt as though I was saying the same things week after week. Then I knew that I was on to something that needed to be presented in a new form that could reach more people than just little ol' me doing my one-on-one consultations every day. I understood that life needed something more from me, and it seemed that the collective was crying out for a new map of self-development and understanding. The time had come for me to bring forth a new piece to the puzzle of human consciousness: understanding our *Fate* on this earth, what it is, and how to transform it into a new energy—*Destiny.*

Through this book I hope you will be able to understand your purpose in ways you've never considered before, while gaining the necessary tools and insights to better dialogue with your soul so that your meaning is made manifest in this world, which so desperately needs your unique grace—your Destiny—to be fulfilled.

INTRODUCTION

Welcome to the Zone of Unlimited Possibility

All of us must struggle with certain things that happen to us, events that occur in spite of our best efforts to be a *good* person and pleasing to the gods of our belief systems. Whether we admit it or not, we still succumb to a belief that if we're good, then bad things won't come our way and the Universe will reward us. Yet every day we see and experience events that call forth our inner victims in protest: "Why me?" or "Why not me?" are questions we've all wailed at one point in life, no?

On December 11, 2005, I found myself asking, "Why her?" when I found out that one of my best friends, Jenny, was killed in a car accident. She was the embodiment of a *good* person. She had a heart of gold, compassion, and empathy that could make you feel heard when you spoke with her. She was as close to her family as it was possible to be and was loved by hundreds of friends. Believe me, I'm not exaggerating—I used to get mad at her for having so many fans because it limited our time together as pals!

Jenny worked as an occupational therapist in a hospital and had picked up an extra shift for the holidays, which put her on the path that led to her death. As she was driving to work that Sunday morning, going only 30 miles an hour on a residential street, she was broadsided by another car that was going the same speed. She had her seatbelt on, and the airbags deployed—all the measures you'd expect would secure your safety in an accident. Although she suffered no major external injuries, somehow the way part of her rib cage was impacted caused her aorta to burst, and she died almost instantly. It was an accident she should have easily survived.

This sent a shock wave through my life, as all sudden deaths do. But the nature of Jenny's passing clearly showed that it was simply her time; her final agreement with Fate had arrived. After her funeral, I went home to visit my folks for the holidays and then returned to my life in Chicago. Three weeks later, I was just beginning to process the loss of my friend when I got a call from my mother, informing me that she'd been involved in a very serious car accident.

While my mom was driving to work with a passenger beside her, their SUV had hit a patch of black ice, causing her to temporarily lose control of the vehicle. One of the tires eventually came off the ice, skidded onto pavement, and then burst, causing the vehicle to roll over three full times before landing on a median.

My mother said that when the SUV finally came to a stop, she'd felt a force of energy enter the car, open the passenger-side door, turn on the interior light, and communicate to her that she was safe and could get out now. It wasn't her time—she had yet to fulfill her Destiny.

Quite frankly, my mother and the passenger with her *should have died.* And Jenny *should have lived.* Even in my shock and grief, I sensed that with this double-shot of synchronicity there was an important message at hand, and these events were part of a bigger design for all of our lives. For my part, I believed that the gods were giving me a way to see something I needed to learn and absorb.

I was left with one crucial question: *How would I change this Fate into Destiny?* This was something that I'd been asked by my soul many, many times before. You've also had this question asked of you many times before—for it's part of the agreement your soul made before incarnating onto this planet for the creative journey called your life.

But while we're here, are we fated or free to choose our path? What is Fate? What is Destiny? How do we know the difference?

When I was 24—years before these two accidents brought the message home to me—I was graced with an experience that incontestably awakened these questions in me. It had been the worst year of my life. After six years in Minneapolis and having finished my collegiate studies, I decided to move to Seattle for a relationship and also to begin my career as an upstart intuitive-astrologer. Once in my new city, things got off to a good start professionally, but my personal life eventually began to take a drastic downturn. As the relationship I'd been involved in slowly disintegrated, so did I.

Although I was a born seeker of life's meaning and felt a larger force guiding me, everything I'd trusted and felt guided toward fell apart that year. Although it was clear by then that I'd been granted incredible skills as an intuitive, I was in shambles. How could I tell people what to do with their lives when mine was such an obvious mess? In addition to my failed relationship, my family was also in crisis. And then clients suddenly stopped coming to my practice, which led me to wonder how I'd make a living. My refrain became: *What do I do now?* Things got so bad that I actually ended up homeless for a brief time, which forced me to move back to Minneapolis.

Once I'd returned to Minnesota, the crisis wasn't over. I was still feeling lost and desperate for revelation, so I prayed for guidance, asking: *What is my purpose? Why am I here on this planet? What will become of my life? Have I been on the wrong track?* Although some of these queries are common for those in their 20s who are searching for a footing in the world, they're also questions that burn in all of us regardless of our age. And the fervor with which we seek the answers is the result of our purpose pursuing us.

Frustrated and desperate, I called out to the Universe: *I've had enough! I don't know what to do. Tell me what to do next to fulfill my destiny.* The answer came in a way I never could have anticipated.

Exhausted by my confusion and frustration, I lay down and slipped into sleep. Somehow, while asleep, I left my body and was led by a presence I couldn't really see (but could sense) through space and time to a scene where a tent was set up on a grassy hill. The unseen presence communicated to me that I should go inside. There I met a "being" of powerful countenance, seated in a chair with two male guardians at her side. She had ice blue eyes that radiated wisdom, and I could sense that she was ancient and full of vision. As she motioned for me to come up to her, she said, "You want to know your future and what your purpose is in this life."

I was in a bit of shock because, hey, I was out of my body, and there was this "being" speaking to me. But I got my bearings and answered, "Yes, I do want to know. Please tell me—I'm lost!"

"Hold out your palms," she commanded. I did, and she seemed to examine them like a palm reader would. Then she looked up and told me, "I can't tell you your future because it's changeable." But then, paradoxically, she took the nail of her index finger—which was razor sharp—and began to cut lines into my palms. This hurt like hell and made my eyes water. And when it was over, she spoke again and said, "I have cut into your hands, your Fate. All you have desired in your deepest being to be in life—you will be. Your agreement with Destiny is set."

I wanted to know more, but before I could ask, I felt myself being pulled through time and space right back into my body. Gasping as if I'd been holding my breath for ten minutes, I opened my eyes. Buzzing with energy, I grabbed my journal and wrote down every detail, knowing that this encounter had been much more than a dream. I have that notebook to this day. I still review it often to remind myself that the encounter really happened and to keep gaining more insight into the experience.

In time, I came to understand what an immense gift I'd been given in that brief meeting with the "being." She'd communicated to me one of the richest paradoxes of life: that we are both *fated* and *free*—that our future is both prewritten and changeable. Our Fate will bring to us everything we need to fulfill our purpose here; but what we do with what Fate gives us, through our creative power of choice, determines our Destiny. This book is, in part, the result of a quest that was launched through that experience—a quest to understand this Divinely ordained paradox and the two forces that fundamentally direct our mortal lives: Fate and Destiny.

Since our first collective breath, human beings have been struggling to establish a deeper understanding of our relationship with our environment, each other, our purpose, and our gods. Modern people—you and me—are often guided by a psychological model that doesn't make room for the soul, by religious paradigms that attach sin to being alive and embodied, or by New Age theories that allege there are no limits to what we can manifest through a positive attitude. The ancients, on the other hand, let their deeper wisdom reveal itself spontaneously through the myths and symbols they created.

Perhaps the most elaborate and celebrated myths in our Western world belonged to the Greeks, who believed that our soul met with three Fates before we were born. These beings assigned us an *allotment*—a specific set of limits that contain and act as a vessel for our purpose in life: our Destiny. The Greeks held that humans must respect and honor the limitations written for them by the Fates. To transgress these boundaries would be an act of hubris, or exaggerated arrogance, and would go against the very fabric of the cosmos, thus invoking the wrath of the gods.

Ancient culture began to shift from a matriarchy and give way to the power structure of patriarchy about 4,000 years ago. At that time, we began to lose touch with the myths that honored the symbolic power of these three female deities as primal forces that regulated the unfolding and purpose of a mortal life. Over time, we forgot that we're each born with a core inscription on our soul that's intended to direct our life's journey.

One supreme God took over through His *Divine Providence*—the power to create a world in seven days and bestow His grace at will without answering to any limits.

This mythic masculine idea of the Almighty replaced the myths of antiquity, relegating them to the status of folklore—imaginative but archaic—and pagan stories taught in classrooms. As we lost a reverence for the Divine Feminine, which had given us an integrated connection to our bodies, natural inner law, and limits—we became a *fate-phobic* culture.

Let's face it: We in the West don't like limitation. Nor do we want to pray to a God Who Himself has limits and lacks supreme will. We don't want to face the possibility that some things are out of our control and that perhaps much of our life has already been predetermined, including the ultimate Fate we'll each face: death. This illusion of control is why some people believe a car is safer than an airplane, despite overwhelming statistics to the contrary. We want to think that anything is possible in our lives—and it is, within the confines of our Fate. And when we bump into those limits, we often cry out that life isn't fair.

Our profound denial of Fate has generated a dominance of victim consciousness in our contemporary psychospiritual and global culture. We can't accept that sometimes things aren't fair. Even in the case of an obvious accident, our litigious culture immediately wants to know who's going to pay for the pain, suffering, and loss that such fated events often bring. And while we struggle for a false sense of justice, our true potential passes us by. We're pushing the soul out of our lives, empowering the victim via demands of recompense based on what Fate brings our way—especially if someone, God forbid, dies. Imagine if we could sue Mother Nature—she'd be filing for bankruptcy! We've lost the much-needed reverence for our limits as mortals.

This has put us at odds with our own inner nature and with Mother Nature as well—disconnecting us from the life force itself, which is the real source of our Destiny and purpose. To us, the word *Fate* conjures up images of death and loss, such as the grim reaper who walks the earth harvesting souls with his deadly sickle. But Fate is so much more than this.

We're fated to our race, to our family, to our place and time of birth—and try as we might, we can't change certain things about our lives. For example, now that I'm on Earth in my 6'1", white, male body, I can't just decide that I'd prefer to be a 5'1" Asian woman. Although I can alter the color or texture of my hair, it's too late to change my race, true gender, or height—that allotment was given to my soul before I came here.

Furthermore, I'm fully aware that I am fated to leave this plane of existence someday. Lest we forget, we do actually die—something not even Botox can fix! In spite of our current gods, mythologies, and objections, Fate is still alive and well. And although we run from it with our plastic surgeons and face creams, we know that it will always catch us in the end.

But what if we learned to honor Fate by surrendering to its limitations as a form of guidance? What if there were ways to forge a conscious relationship with these restrictions? What if we could use the things that happen to us as arrows pointing us toward a new horizon of yet-to-be-lived potential? Would we then truly unlock our Destiny and place another piece into the puzzle of our Universe? Fate manifests in many different forms, but always asks us a question: *What will you do with what I've given to you?* How we each answer is what shapes our Destiny.

Through my work as an intuitive consultant over the past ten years, I've come to understand what that wise "being" in the tent was trying to tell me: Before incarnation, each person makes two agreements with the Universe. One is with Fate, one with Destiny.

We agree first, with Fate, to be threads woven into the fabric of the cosmos . . . its cycles, rhythm, timing, and laws. The moments of our first breaths fuse us with a matrix of family, social, national, and global psychic energies. For the rest of our lives, this Fate and its energies pour into the ocean of our being like tributaries, greatly impacting our self-concept, empowerment, health, and quality of life.

We work next with Destiny, forming an agreement that has the potential to unlock the fullest and most satisfying expression of our being. It demands that we birth a new consciousness that allows the soul greater authority in our personality, or ego. With an ego/soul connection, we're empowered to play the hand we were dealt by Fate with integrity, grace, humility, compassion, courage, honor, wit, spontaneity, genius, and reverence.

It's a dance of opposites, a balance of light and shadow, and in order to master it, we must become truly conscious and comfortable with both partners. I've written this book to serve as a fundamental guide, aid, and catalyst in forging a relationship with your Fate. Through opening and unfolding to the allotment given to you and understanding how you can unconsciously fate yourself into unnecessarily sabotaging your true potential, you'll begin to open the space between your Fate and your Destiny, *the zone of truly unlimited possibility.*

As you move further into this book, I'll give you many necessary tools to aid you in accessing this place where Fate transforms into Destiny through the power of your choices—your authentic free will. You'll learn to discern what you *can* change and what you can't, yet must respect and honor. You'll discover that it's in honoring your Divinely designed circumference that you'll find your center, and through this that you can change the world.

It's my intention that you'll gain a new model for perceiving your life's purpose and discover your true potential. If you're holding this book in your hands right now, you're ready and it's time.

PART I

TOOLS FOR TRANSFORMING FATE INTO DESTINY

During the early years of my professional work as an intuitive, I began to detect two fundamental forces that seemed to dance together in the creation of our lives. Observing the many ways these energies worked with different clients led me to conclude that, prior to birth, each human soul seemed to have met with celestial guardians of Earth and established two agreements with them and the Universe that must be fulfilled as part of the human experience—one with Fate and one with Destiny. Taken together, these comprise what I call our Cosmic Contract. In order to fulfill that contract and consciously co-create our lives (by *co-create* I mean working through our consciousness and power of choice in tandem with the Divine), we must wield some important and powerful tools.

Oftentimes, the quality of the tools we employ can determine the measure of what we create. Therefore, before we begin to examine *your* agreement with Fate and how to transform that into Destiny, it's crucial that you read and assimilate the concepts presented in this section:

- Acceptance
- Authentic Choice
- Surrender
- Prayer
- The Law of Attraction

I've organized their order intentionally to demonstrate the general sequence in which they're most often and constructively applied to your Fate.

You'll be taking these tools with you as you investigate your agreements with Fate, so you can transform them into something life affirming. These are essential instruments of Destiny that you must understand deeply before you can fulfill your Cosmic Contract. You simply can't do it without them.

You'll often find that your Fate can manifest in situations where perhaps only one, two, or three of these items may be necessary for your Destiny to come alive. Nonetheless, many times you'll need to use all of them to distill the hidden blessings found in your limitations and challenges. Simply put, what follows is an explanation of your Cosmic Contract and the tools essential for an empowered life.

Chapter 1

THE SOUL'S TWO AGREEMENTS—YOUR COSMIC CONTRACT

Your Cosmic Contract with Fate and Destiny governs the way your life unfolds and asks that you fulfill the agreements that you made prior to coming here. But what exactly are the terms? Although both Fate and Destiny are equal parts comprising the whole of your purpose, let's look at Fate first—as I've discovered that it's the first agreement our souls made with the Universe and the guardians of this planet.

Your Agreement with Fate

First of all, what the heck is Fate? I don't know about you, but I hear people mixing up the terms Fate and Destiny all the time as if they're the same thing. While I'm going to be expanding the meaning of the term throughout the entire book, I want to give you a basic understanding on which to build. For now, I'll define

Fate as *that which has been predetermined and written into our life's contract before we were born, which comes into our existence on many levels and in many different forms, but primarily serves as the vessel and structure through which our Destiny is fulfilled and contained.*

In other words, the soul makes a primary agreement that includes the acceptance of certain necessary terms as part of the human journey. For example, your soul agreed to the Fate of incarnating into your body, gender, race, culture, appearance, and family of origin as the perfect setup for your life's purpose.

This idea that before we're born we meet with Earth guardians who interface with our spiritual guides and our soul in order to devise a creative journey on this planet was actually first articulated thousands of years ago in Plato's "The Myth of Er." Plato and the ancient Greeks called these guardians the three Fates, goddesses responsible for scripting our lives before we arrive on the planet.

In *The Republic,* Plato recounts the story of a soldier named Er. From a modern-day perspective, this man had what we'd recognize as a near-death experience. Killed in battle, his body was just about to be burned on a funeral pyre when he suddenly came back to life! He had much to tell of his time in the afterlife, for he'd been allowed to witness the operation of the death–rebirth cycle of incarnation (a cycle to which all souls eventually must return). He described the threshold of rebirth as a liminal (in-between) space in which each soul meets with the three Fates.

These three deities—Clotho, the spinner; Lachesis, the measurer; and Atropos, the cutter—were among the first beings ever created out of the Chaos (the Greek equivalent to the spirit world). They were older than all the other gods and reigned supreme in the pantheon. They decreed that each must keep to his or her lot, which was an assigned contract or limitation given to each according to the god's role in the Universe. Zeus could not be Hades; he was fated as a sky god. Aphrodite could never be Apollo; it was not her lot. Similarly, neither you nor I can be someone else we're not fated to be.

Er watched as these white-robed "Daughters of Necessity" designed the incarnate contracts of all heavenly and earthly beings. Woven into each design were certain limitations, prescripted events serving as soul lessons based on prior incarnations and the length of each individual's life. Most important, the Fates gave all mortals inner designs and templates to guide them toward what they were meant to become and experience.

Based on my experiences with clients, I sense that Plato was really on to something fundamental to understanding our mortal journey, if we translate this myth into insight for our modern times. Mainly, we must embrace that a choice was indeed made when our soul met with the guardians of Earth, a decision to be bound to a contract with Fate. The ego often finds this baffling once we're here. How many of us have looked at our lives and wondered, *Why didn't I pick the lot of Bill Gates?* Yet when we try to be something other that what our inner design dictates, we fate ourselves to an unfulfilled life of suffering.

That's why we must understand that this level of choice is made prior to incarnation and originates from the intentions of our immortal soul. Dialoguing with the soul is urgent and necessary if we're to discover what the agreements are, for it's within them that our purpose is found.

It can be challenging when we discover that the choices our soul made before birth often are painful for our personality/ego to absorb and accept. As we live in a world of duality (dark/light, pain/pleasure, good/bad, and so forth), the mortal part of us grasps that which feels best, no? This creates the struggle we all experience as we continually wrestle with the apparent dualism of Earth. Initially, it can be quite painful for the personality to absorb that the soul likes to awaken us to its presence through the contrast offered by polarities such as pain and pleasure. Therefore, to fully appreciate the intentions of our soul and its contract with Fate, we must be willing to relinquish the dualistic ideas of the ego such as fair/unfair, right/wrong, and good/evil so that we can unleash our Destiny.

Suffering and duality, as the Buddha taught, are part of the agreement that Fate often brings to our soul's journey in this world, and only when we include them in our understanding of human consciousness are we complete. Buddhism also teaches (as do many other spiritual traditions) that liberation comes when we embrace the middle path and stop grasping for pleasure and pushing away pain. Until we begin to look at the Fate of our mortal lives with the eyes of the soul, we remain chained to the suffering produced by polarizing into these opposites.

With that said, although there are many types of Fate to explore, throughout this book I'm going to teach you how to identify your agreement with Fate in two primary ways and present you with the necessary tools you'll need to transform them both into Destiny.

— **Mortal Fate:** This is the Fate that you often can't change. It was written into your soul before you came here, and you must live it out as part of your Destiny. It often manifests as conditions and events that are out of your control. These may have been chosen by your soul as necessary experiences of spiritual awakening. This Fate includes the expiration date we're all given: our death. Although many of us currently live in constant denial that we're aging and will one day head back whence we came, we all must humbly bow before this. It spares no one—that's why I call it your Mortal Fate. It also deals with many other layers of earthly limitation that each of us must negotiate as human beings: genetics, ethnicity, race, gender, and appearance, to name just a few. Many of these things we can't alter, but simply have to work within as part of our mortal experience. We must also embrace another sort of meeting with death: the loss of a loved one. Pretty morbid, I know, but none of us on Earth is getting out of here alive!

— **Self Fate:** This is the Fate you unconsciously create in drawing ego-fueled, self-made trials to yourself. These challenges are often the by-product of going against your inner design when you try to be or become something you're not meant to be, or when you don't own and integrate parts of your nature that are seeking acknowledgment and/or incarnate expression. We'll be investigating this process deeply, as well as looking at how you enchain yourself to the wheel of suffering by the ways you unwittingly empower a polarization of opposites within yourself. I'll teach you how this may produce more suffering—more Fate—in your life.

That said, let's look at the lighter side of your Cosmic Contract, which is your agreement to transform both

Mortal and Self Fate into Destiny. To do that, we must recognize Destiny as your soul's second agreement with the Universe.

Your Agreement with Destiny

The word *Destiny* is derived from the Latin verb *destino,* from which we derive our English words *destination, design,* and *destine.* Destiny is *learning to work with your challenges so that you can be who and what you truly are (because there's simply nothing else you can be), and then yoking this "being" into service to the collective world or others around you.*

Destiny is where you get to create with the Divine by using the powers at your disposal within your Fate. Although Destiny demands the actualization of your potential and the fullest expression of your essence, it's never completed because it's like the transitive verb of life, whereas Fate acts as the noun. In other words, Destiny is the *doing,* Fate is the *being,* and both dance together—forming the sentences, paragraphs, and stories of our journey as human beings.

In simpler terms, Destiny is that which you create within the boundaries of the Fate you're given. It issues forth from what was written on your soul before you incarnated and matures into this world as you become who you were born to be, learning how to manage the power of choice and the Law of Attraction.

You may have heard that Fate is the hand of cards that life deals you, and Destiny is how you play it. This means that through your soul's agreement with Destiny, you must *transform* your Fate into something more life affirming, thus leaving this world a better place. Destiny is your capacity to live out the threads of your Fate in a unique way that *only you* can do, while having a positive vibrational impact on the world's energy and soul.

Intuitively Reading Your Cosmic Contract

If I do an intuitive reading for you, I'm able to access the terms of your agreements with Fate and Destiny. As I focus and tune in to you, I enter into the larger matrix of Universal consciousness. My intuition then provides me with various symbolic impressions that communicate to my mind various components of your contract. I get a sense of what your soul came to experience, what gifts it has innately brought into life, and what major challenges it must work with to create an affirming journey on this planet.

In addition, I connect to your *team*—spirit guides and teachers who are always around and coaching you via your own intuition. These are the same ones who helped you forge your Cosmic Contract before you incarnated. By reading your agreement and working with your team, I'm able to offer helpful guidance on how you can best participate in your contract with Fate. By understanding and consciously working with the terms that have been set, Fate can become Destiny. Once that occurs, it begins to sustain the motion of your life—cutting down all obstacles on your path like a noble warrior so that you can fulfill your purpose.

As I guide you forward through this book, I'm hopeful that our journey together will catalyze an investigation of these two forces so that you're empowered to fulfill your soul's agreement with them—transforming your Fate into Destiny. I'll do my best to impart to you what the gods have given me by teaching you fundamental tools that you can apply to each challenging circumstance and event that occurs—tools that unlock your highest potential.

One thing I'm sure of: Coming to Earth is an opportunity that the soul finds unquestionably worthy of the pain and illusory separateness we experience here. It knows that this opportunity demands an agreement with Fate that includes certain necessary terms as part of our journey. But what exactly is the soul's intention in forging a Cosmic Contract and coming to this planet anyway? I don't know about you, but I can't count the number of times I've asked myself, *What the hell was my soul thinking?*

The Soul's Intention

A couple of years ago while teaching an intensive weekend workshop on the intuitive uses of astrology, I was discussing the way in which the soul fuses with the Earth dimension through the birth process. This was a complex concept and key to this particular workshop. I was going into specifics regarding certain patterns and roles the soul may be bound to within a family (such as being the emotional scapegoat), when a student raised her hand.

"Robert," she began, "when we die, what happens to the patterns we've been born into regarding our family? I mean, when we go, do we take those with us?"

I was stunned. In all my years of teaching and interpreting the world of the soul and its intention, I'd never thought of this before. I was also intrigued and wondered to myself, *How does that work?* Instantly, I received an intuitive impression that has forever changed my understanding. I saw the soul as a sphere of light consciousness descending to Earth and fusing with the patterns and conditions of this dimension that are cosmic, global, national, cultural, and familial. Then I perceived it leaving them behind when departing the body and Earth, yet the soul was more luminous than before the incarnate experience—as if its energy had been enlightened. These patterns, such as alcoholism, are not part of the soul as I'd previously conceived of them. Instead, they're conditions the soul merges with for certain purposes, based on its creative intention *in this lifetime.*

This intuitive impression took only a moment, yet it communicated so much information, including a clear answer to my student's question: No, we do *not* take the patterns of a lifetime with us when we pass from this plane into the nonphysical dimension. They're separate and distinct from the soul. Instead, we retain only the experiences related to the raising of our vibration and luminosity. In other words, it's as if the soul thrives and expands its consciousness through creation itself, regardless of the journey it has taken in this world. Yet paradoxically, all experiences and memories from this and other lifetimes are recorded as part of a spiritual archive—whether they happened here on Earth or somewhere else.

And one of the most striking things I sense through my intuitive work is that there are many, many places and dimensions where your soul might have chosen to incarnate and has done so in the past. In our mundane, earthbound lives, we often forget that this is a massive universe. Astronomers tell us that the average galaxy is a colossal island of 100 billion (or more) stars, and there are most likely at least 50 billion galaxies in this universe alone—and that's a minimum estimate. Furthermore, that unfathomable vastness may be only a speck in a cosmos containing millions of universes! With such a diverse and expansive array of possibilities, it just doesn't make sense that this planet would be the only place your soul has visited, does it?

But the soul seems to like coming to Earth to create and learn through the polarity of opposites found here. This allows it to expand itself vibrationally as it comes to know itself via experiences of contrast.

That said, what exactly *is* the soul? And furthermore, how does it differ from the spirit, and how does each fit into the whole of our consciousness? Before you begin the task of consciously transforming your Fate into Destiny, let's define some key terms—often given various meanings—that you'll need to understand on our journey together through this book.

In addition, I strongly recommend that you get a journal specifically for working with this book. In the chapters to come, there are various exercises to help you clearly identify different facets of your Fate, and I'll ask you to assess and write about various aspects of your life. Not to mention, the mere act of reading will surely inspire many thoughts and questions you'll want to jot down! And as you'll soon see, this journal will become a profound way for you to dialogue with your soul.

Coming to Know the Soul

Soul . . . sit with that word for a minute and experience it for yourself. Repeat it slowly: *soul.* What feeling does it evoke within you? When I say the word to myself, I feel a sense of being, stillness, and timelessness. For me, the soul is the part of consciousness that's much greater than my personal sense of identity. It's our total being and essence, the eternal part of us that's omniscient, immortal, and multidimensional. We may hear the soul referred to as the deeper, higher, or inner self; in my experience, it's *all* of these and more.

The soul is the repository of all our creative journeys, containing every experience of each of our lifetimes. It's feminine in function—meaning that it contains, receives, and just rests in simply being. In contrast, the spirit is the more masculine aspect of our consciousness that's active and vested in becoming.

Our soul is the consciousness that chose to experience creation through our name, identity, and participation in this world. But although the soul is an aspect of awareness, we can't fully comprehend its nature with our minds because it transcends our thinking; yet we can approach it and even come to know it through deep mystical introspection and experience.

Coming to know your soul is fundamental to the fulfillment of your purpose in this life. This aspect of your being contains the core inscription created for your life, a unique blueprint that was preconceived and written before your descent to Earth. If you don't become acquainted with your soul, you won't be able to discover this writing within you, leaving you vulnerable to being manipulated by external forces in this world. In other words, if you don't access direction from within, your life will be directed from without. This vulnerability could derail your Destiny—your creative task of fulfilling your highest potential in this lifetime—as you become whatever this world makes of you, instead of "soul-made."

So why did this greater part of us enlist in Earth school? Why are we here? I used to think, as many others do, that our time on this planet is a function of evolution and karma—you know, because we have things to learn, karmic debts to pay. But after experiencing the clarity of that brief vision that I mentioned earlier, I came to understand that we're here because we have things *to experience and to create.*

I know now that the soul, our deepest being, raises its luminosity and consciousness by participating in the expansive unfolding of the Universe itself. I understand now that with each lifetime, this aspect of our being experiences creation via the incarnation in which it participates. And Earth is just one stop of many on our soul's cosmic creative journey.

In client readings, I sense that many people are "new here"—that their souls aren't used to being born into our earthly realm where things are extremely dense and where energy transforms into matter very slowly. Conversely, there are those whom I call "Earth souls" because I sense that they've been here many times before, seeming almost to be a part of the planet's higher self.

I also sense that we come here with others that are part of our soul group. This is composed of our cosmic companions whom we've taken other incarnate journeys with and who tend to be going through similar creative experiences with us. You've most likely come to know many members of your soul group already. They sometimes show up as our parents, siblings, and friends; or they can be those you've just met whom you seem to already *know,* much like a sense of déjà vu. In fact, we could also call these individuals "soul mates."

The head mentors of our group often incarnate as our greatest teachers in this lifetime. I should also mention that some members can show up as adversaries, having formed a contract with you that requires them to push you to grow through conflict! However, I also sense that not all members of our soul group incarnate with us; some remain on the other side and act as guardian angels.

Whether we're in this dimension with those from our group or somewhere else that we can't even imagine, there's something that seems to pulse through all of creation—the masculine complement to the feminine soul: the spirit. How do these forces work together in our consciousness?

The Spirit

Spirit is the animating energy that manifests in all of creation. It has also been called *prana, chi,* or *life force.* The word *spirit* is often used interchangeably with the word *soul,* but they're different things. Spirit is a force of energy that connects with intention in the creation of all life. When our spirit is broken, our best intentions are also dashed and our energy is diminished. Those with bright spirits carry within them the vitality of positive vibrations and affirming intentions through which they direct the life force itself, enlivening everything and everyone they touch.

You could say that spirit is the soul's energy *in action* through *the power of intention.* Soul is the container, and spirit is the life force that moves through it, fueled by our focus—the manifestation of our active will to create something. Although the immortal soul and spirit complement each other, neither can get too far without a temporary container that can interface with this world of time and space. That vessel is the mortal ego, which gives shape to your personality.

The Ego—Friend or Foe?

The ego has gotten a bad rap. Contrary to modern Western thinking, it isn't inherently negative. In fact, without it, our soul could never manifest its consciousness in this world. Furthermore, the ego is the fundamental creative tool of the soul within this dimension. You could think of the soul as the writer of reality, and the ego is the pen that inks the higher self's energy onto the paper of the world.

Still, many Western teachers, interpreting Eastern wisdom through their cultural bias, claim that our primary task in spiritual development is the destruction of the ego. Ironically, it's only the ego (which is, in part, your mind) that can comment on the destruction of itself! Nevertheless, this isn't really what Eastern philosophy teaches. Rather, Buddhism, Sufism, and yoga communicate: *Make your ego so expansive through your compassion that it encompasses and includes the soul—your connection to the all that is, your connection to eternity.* How would we write the passions of our greater being onto this world without a pen? Our fundamental task is to construct the best tool possible so that we can bring the soul into the story of life.

I define the ego as the largely conscious part of your personality that's derived from interfacing with the environment around you and that acts to preserve your self-concept and self-esteem as they're formed by that environment. When we begin to believe that we're separate from others, the Divine, and our own soul, the ego is hijacked by the illusion that true power emanates from this manifest world, rather than the soul. The ego then asserts an agenda based on survival fear and self-esteem derived largely from the approval of culture and the people we interact with. When this happens, our soul range is dramatically decreased, rendering us mostly *cultural beings,* instead of living in accordance with our true potential as *celestial beings*—not to mention that we start writing horror stories instead of love stories.

Unfortunately, examples of this flourish in our world, which is obsessed with celebrity worship and consumerism. There are those in our culture who are conspicuous in their desperate need to possess *things,* and they project power and status onto those belongings in order to feel empowered. You may see them driving their Hummers (aka "Earth destroyers") or wearing Prada. To many of us, it seems like an arrogant crime to drive such a large vehicle in the face of our environmental crisis and an oil shortage, and to be so disconnected from the suffering of others as to wear clothes that cost $3,000 while children die in Africa. Still, we each must assess where we believe cultural validation comes from and the power we falsely believe can be acquired from an outer source. Who among us *hasn't* derived an ego boost from a house, a car, or a new outfit? I know that I have! Furthermore,

I'm not saying that there's necessarily something completely wrong with it.

Nonetheless, we must ask ourselves, *Does driving an ostentatious gas-guzzler help write an environmental horror story or a love story in this world? Does wearing designer clothing connect us to each other or deepen divisive class distinctions? Are we honoring our soul or ego with our perceptions of power as something we must source externally through possessions such as these?*

What if we all made the choice to drive hybrid cars instead or to wear clothes by designers that donate a percentage of their profits to combatting AIDS in Africa? Would we then get our egos on board with our souls? The point here is that we get into trouble when we fail to bundle in a deeper sense of soulful identity and mistake the ego as being the center of our consciousness.

But the ego can also become a creative ally when it's in proper relationship to the soul. In other words, while we're here on this planet, we need the ego to house our identity and give us a self-concept separate from everything else. But to write our love stories into the world, we need to remember that we're paradoxically still part of—and have a responsibility to—the greater world. How do we accomplish this? We develop a way to continually dialogue with our soul, always allowing it more influence in our lives. We must develop the discipline of asking ourselves daily: *Am I someone with a soul that possesses an ego, or someone with an ego that possesses a soul?*

Dialoguing with the Soul

Dialoguing with the soul is a lifelong process. It demands that we be able to continually restructure our ego and perceptions in ways that allow our soul new pathways of incarnation into our identity, into our lives. This book is dedicated to teaching you various ways to do just that. The greatest keys to the process of soul dialogue are developing humility and not believing so earnestly in the character we're playing out through our personality.

Without humility, we become arrogant and create Self Fate. But true humbleness has nothing to do with not having a deep sense of value for ourselves; rather, it suspends a sense of entitlement or ego-based privilege that acts as a mask for our greater insecurities. In fact, coming to know your true value is also becoming aware of your Divinity—your soul—which means that you'll have to sacrifice a good/bad, right/wrong, better/worse paradigm of reality and embrace equality, forgiveness, acceptance, and letting go.

Very critical to fulfilling our Destiny is realizing that part of our pre-incarnate plans may have included that we suffer certain hardships and challenges. These are Divinely designed to make our character surface so that it can fuse into our co-creative process, in which spirit flows through us as active energy animated by our intentions. These manifest through our ego, which is why we must work diligently to yoke it to our soul.

So ego, or our personal sense of who we are, may include the soul identity or not. This is based upon how much we're willing to work toward knowing this deepest part of ourselves. Giving up insecurities and privilege can be a rough journey, yet at times it's necessary to gain greater awareness. The sacrifice pays off when the ego and soul are in harmony, for that is when our Destiny is realized.

That said, as I began to understand the dynamic process of birthing onto this planet from years of working with clients and a few of my own mystical experiences, I realized that some old definitions for certain words that circulate in spiritual circles had become obsolete. For example, many students have asked me at workshops how the idea of karma fits into a paradigm where the soul incarnates for creative reasons, not punitive ones.

A Different View of Karma

Karma is defined by Merriam-Webster as "the force generated by a person's actions held in Hinduism and Buddhism to perpetuate transmigration and in its ethical consequences to determine the nature of the person's next existence." In addition, you've probably heard it described as a cycle of "payback" that embraces everything we think, say, and do. If we give up eye-for-an-eye and cause-and-effect versions of justice, then what do we do with the idea of karma?

Although there's certainly a cause-and-effect law in motion in this Universe, reducing karma to a punitive system in which we somehow pay for our actions or sins is a complete misunderstanding of its complexity. It's easy to see the Western Judeo-Christian influence in the interpretation of this Eastern concept: In fact, I once heard someone say that the only difference between this idea and hell seems to be the location!

When it comes to karma we must go deeper than the basic notion that what we did in a past incarnation equates to this life's suffering or pleasure—this is far too myopic. In my work, I've found that one person may have a contract in this existence to absorb another person's karma. For example, I did a reading for a man who'd struggled for 20 years with alcoholism and couldn't figure out why he ended up the failure of his family, while all his siblings were able to live productive lives. His need to understand this brought him to me.

As I conducted his session, I perceived that his soul had chosen to absorb this pattern of addiction, which had been a legacy in the family psyche on his father's side for generations. Meanwhile, his sacrifice allowed his brothers and sisters to flourish as functioning adults—a gift that his soul had contracted to give them because, as the reading showed, it was the only one strong enough to heal the addiction and break the pattern for future descendants. In other words, by taking on this burden as his Fate and breaking it, he gave his family members the gift of Destiny and healed the legacy.

In another example, an environmentalist friend once told me that someone had said her heartfelt motivation to heal the earth was the result of having been so destructive to the environment in another life. Put off by this punitive interpretation, I offered her an alternative picture: "Perhaps you were a Native American in a past life and loved the land so deeply that you brought that connection with you in this lifetime."

When it comes to karma and the way it weaves into the concepts in this book, what I sense is this: Whatever we did in a past life was an act of creation based on beliefs we contained in our ego about ourselves, the Universe, and the Divine. One of the many reasons we're here now is to create anew in this lifetime. And yes, perhaps some of our past efforts weren't too pretty. So instead of coming back to Earth as a form of punishment for those deeds, let's imagine that we've chosen to challenge the core beliefs that led to them, the ones that served as the creative tools our soul used previously.

In addition, let's define beliefs as thought-forms we engage in over and over again until they become patterns. Before incarnation, we must first plan the general structure of our lifetime so that it challenges those ideas. This means that we're going to ask to be assigned situations that will force on us the consequences of our past conceptions so that they can be dismantled—and this is when our past karma shows up as a form of Fate. It's also how the soul awakens the ego to create in more affirming ways via polarity. In other words, to start learning how to work through compassion, we must come to know its opposite (judgment) first, but not as a form of punishment. Rather, it's a creative awakening.

The specifics of how necessary situations are planned and scripted to bring about our awareness of other options are really irrelevant. It's the belief that's the issue, not necessarily what we've done in a past life because of it. To illustrate this, let's say you were put into a position of power in a past incarnation and you abused it through controlling, lying, manipulating the public, and killing those who threatened your dominance. What's at issue, then, is the core belief and perception that you were *powerless,* and that real might came from controlling others. That's what motivated your choices and defined your creative contribution to the Universe in that existence. The ego had been hijacked by illusion, and little realization of the soul could occur. So you died, and during your past-life review on the other side, you gasped and begged to be given a chance to create a different experience in your next incarnation. As such, the compassionate Universe assigned you a journey in which you'd have to come to terms with the belief of being powerless.

How that would be scripted only the Fates could tell because there are so many other threads to consider as you are woven into *everything* in the Universe. All existence is connected at the level of quantum energy; all is, indeed, One. Therefore, in each lifetime your own soul's creative need to evolve would have to be woven into the larger fabric of cosmic evolution. It's a complex process no mortal could even conceive of!

Nonetheless, once you've faced the consequences of a belief, you can choose what you want to do about it—wherever you incarnate. This is part of Destiny. You could decide to ignore the consequences and refuse to release the limiting notion, opting to fate yourself to more unhappiness. But I'm hopeful that you'll choose to dump it and create a new one that better serves your soul's intention and desire to create in more expansive and life-affirming ways that honor how you're part of the whole web of creation.

Given this new understanding of karma, can we reduce all that happens in a human lifetime to a simplistic punishment for past transgressions? Now I know you just said "No!" If there's one thing I've learned through my work, it's that the soul's agenda often doesn't make sense to our mortal minds. Life is anything but fair, but it's always creative. That's why it can feel as if we're living our own trials of Job when trouble strikes. *Why am I fated to live this way? Why did this happen to me?* we lament, shaking our fists at the heavens.

While questions like these often arise naturally out of the vicissitudes of human life, we're going to need some important and powerful tools to get past the victim inside who holds us hostage, especially if we're going to transform our Fate into Destiny. We'll look at those tools in the next chapter.

Chapter 2

ACCEPTANCE AND AUTHENTIC CHOICE

The first two tools for transforming Fate into Destiny—acceptance and authentic choice—work somewhat in tandem. Nothing can move the energy of our lives, turning tragedies into blessings, the way the power of acceptance can. But coming to acceptance doesn't happen overnight. It requires that we work through many complex feelings—anger, shame, guilt, jealousy, rage, regret, grief, and self-loathing—and paradoxically we can't begin to do this until we accept them, too!

Authentic choice, or free will, is more complex than we might first assume—and more powerful. There is, perhaps, no act more creative than making a choice. It distributes your life force through the consequences, making it your fundamental creative tool. You might even say that it trumps acceptance, because we must first choose to accept! But nothing in our lives can truly change unless we first come to terms with it "as is," so let's look at acceptance first.

Accepting a Way Out of Victim Consciousness

Acceptance often takes time. Until then, we're anchored to what we resist—it remains a "stuck" part of our reality, one that will continue to sabotage our lives. We must even accept our faults, for fighting them only strengthens them. Each of us has struggled with certain events, tragedies, accidents, and people. If you can't acknowledge that some are there by Divine design, you'll be held hostage by victim consciousness for a lifetime.

Again and again, I've seen this to be the case for my clients, especially when it comes to the Fate we experience in our family of origin. This was profoundly revealed by a client reading that clearly demonstrates how acceptance can change the course of our lives in an instant. Paul was 42 years old when he came to me for assistance because he was tired of being "done wrong" by life. He had a really hard time seeing the world as just, and expended a lot of energy fighting as an advocate for fairness. This passion led him to become a lawyer—a profession that he ultimately came to despise.

While I was intuitively reading Paul in preparation for our meeting, I could sense that he was a gay man and had been sexually abused by his father. I also read his Cosmic Contract and discerned that in this lifetime, he needed to find ways to create value for himself by healing his victim consciousness.

As we sat down for the session, I communicated some of my basic philosophy that we're fated to our parents and certain experiences as children. This immediately triggered a response him, and I saw his face flush red with anger. He said that he'd been so severely sexually abused by his father that he'd blocked out conscious memory of it. He only discovered the experience through hypnotic regressive therapy.

"Robert," he challenged, "can you sit there and tell me that I *chose* a father who would do such a thing?" In that moment, it was clear to me that Paul hadn't yet truly *accepted* what had happened to him. I could only see a little boy in front of me, speaking through both his inner victim and child. I asked Paul to just sit with the idea that his soul had chosen this as a Fate through which his Destiny could be born—but only if he could come to terms with it first.

Later in the reading, we talked about Paul's life as a gay man. He told me that when the AIDS crisis first hit in the early 1980s, he'd been celibate for a number of years because he had no desire for sex, but wasn't sure why his libido was so low. This had led him to the hypnotic regressive therapy to figure out why—and this was where he remembered his father's abuse. But it was because of this psycho-sexual block that he'd survived the first wave of the AIDS epidemic. You see, during the time when no one knew how the HIV virus was transmitted and was spreading, he simply wasn't having any sex.

I sat back in my chair and asked Paul if he'd ever considered that his father's sexual abuse had, in truth, saved his life. Was it somehow integral to his purpose? At first, unable to breathe or speak, he couldn't answer me. But then tears filled his eyes and began to pour down his cheeks. As he wept, I could see years of resentment and victimization washing away, flowing out of his being as he finally accepted that his childhood Fate just might have served a greater purpose.

In that moment, Paul's sense of victimization was replaced with acceptance. He was forever changed, and shortly after our reading, he quit practicing law in order to become a licensed counselor for abused children. Through the power of acceptance, he transformed the Fate of his early years into Destiny.

Acceptance is crucial in the fulfillment of our agreement with Destiny, for it is only through acceptance that we move from victimization to an *initiation* into our soul's purpose. We're then able to incarnate a new quality of our consciousness. We can live within earthly paradoxes in an empowered way as we move beyond a sense of entitlement that life should always be fair. Acceptance allows us to find the silver lining within our Fate, which moves us back into the flow of our Destiny, opening our lives up to new options. At that point, we're ready to consciously use the next tool: *the power of authentic choice.*

Authentic Choice

Acceptance opens us up to a plethora of new choices, and this is when we must focus on authentic choice. Moreover, all the wonderful philosophies and disciplines we can cultivate in pursuit of virtue have but one end: the moment of choice. Each time this happens, the Divine asks us two crucial questions that invite us to bring forth our highest potential: Will we choose to affirm life and our interconnectedness in the decisions we make? Or will we opt to affirm the illusion of separateness, negating the supreme spiritual law that All is One?

These fundamental questions are the basis of most spiritual and religious teachings, which want to help us affirm our connection to the Divine and each other through the choices we make every day. Many faith traditions teach us not to harm, kill, or abuse others for any reason—because what you do to another, you do to yourself and to God.

The word *religion* itself carries this message. It's derived from the Latin *religio,* which means to "reconnect" or "reunite"—to tie back together. This shows that this was, in fact, the original goal of these organizations: to join humanity with the heavenly in a conscious rapport and to yoke our human will with the Divine.

Every day we're confronted with choices from the moment we wake up until we lay down our heads at night—and every choice asks us to confront what we truly value. What we choose will always point toward what we hold dear in our hearts, no matter what we say our philosophies are. Values define how we live and what we choose.

That said, how do we form our values? Are they even truly our own, or are they handed down by our culture or parents and then unconsciously adopted? If we make choices based on what others hold dear, things that don't resonate with our soul's integrity, just how free are we? What exactly *is* free will? I think by now you're beginning to see just how complex the concept of choice truly is. Let's dive in a bit deeper and investigate the development of authentic choice and free will.

Fate and Free Will

"Free will is the ability to do gladly that which I must do."
— C. G. Jung

If I were to define *free will,* I'd say that it's *the ability to choose, unaffected by mental habits, irrational or unconscious desires, familial and cultural bias, emotional states, addictions, or the restraints of physical or Divinely imposed necessity or volition.* Simply put, it means taking a course of action that we *solely* intend. With that in mind, when—if ever—do we make choices based only on our own intentions? Does free will even exist?

The answer isn't as simple as yes or no. Although we do have some measure of independence, we aren't at liberty in all things. Free will operates at varying degrees, depending on circumstances. For example, I can't just wake up tomorrow and decide that I'd like to see the sun rise in the West and set in the East. But I could have chosen not to write this book, and you could have opted not to buy it. Yet here we are, which tells us that choice does indeed exist.

But why do we make certain selections? You see, to go with what we value most in our hearts, the question isn't really *Do we have the option of making choices?* Rather, it becomes *Where are we free to choose, what influences the decisions we make, why do we pick certain options, and what role do our choices play in the transformation of our Fate into Destiny?*

As you now know, we're here because of our soul's decision to come to this planet and experience a heroic journey of co-creation. But by the time we've descended to Earth, certain choices have already been irrevocably made. They constitute our agreement with Fate and set up the options we're going to be presented with in this lifetime that will test us and ultimately determine how we fulfill our agreement with Destiny.

To be empowered in this process, we need to learn just how choice works, and doing so requires an awareness of our limitations. We must understand that the freedom we have in free will is to align with our inner design, but we don't have the liberty to be anything other than who we're meant to become. Said another way, each of us eventually awakens to the terrifying reality that there is precious little we can truly control in life—that is, our ego is the caboose on the train of our being, and the soul is the engine that's truly in charge of our lives. The ego must humbly learn that it can only control the quality of our journey, not the destination, which was planned before we came here. The only real choice we have is this: *Do I want to travel with a smile or a frown on my face?*

This question is more complicated than it seems at first glance because many times our choices aren't really made *by* us, but *for* us—unconsciously. We often travel to the various destinations assigned for our life with grumpy faces. Our egos are unknowingly under spells that cause us to seek happiness by trying to control the things we can't, which in turn influences what we choose.

Nonetheless, we all begin our human development through our ego. So moving toward choices of Destiny requires that we put time and effort into the continual restructuring of our values and ego. This demands the development of something I call *inner authority,* which is a soul strength birthed into our ego structure as we grow into adulthood and find our deepest sense of authenticity.

Initiations into Authenticity

"Free will is the will not to conform to the past, and is the measure of a man's capacity to act as an individual."
— Dane Rudhyar, astrologer, author, and composer

After years of working with hundreds of people, I began to see that each of us has our own schedule of growth and development that's uniquely timed according to our purpose. Still, we all experience common thresholds that require us to ask two crucial questions: *Where does the majority of my self-concept come from? Is that serving my soul's destination?*

These turning points arrive whether we're ready or not. They further our empowerment, most often manifesting as relationships that must end; job loss or dissatisfaction (or conversely, sudden success and new responsibilities); finally dealing with past abuse; or major changes within the structure of our family of origin. Whatever catalyzes our entry into greater self-mastery, we're assigned the task of beginning anew the work of birthing ourselves out of the matrix of our past through our own efforts. At this point, the ego—or self-concept—must be developed and strengthened in new ways. The *old* ego, which has become untenable to the soul's agenda, must be restructured. I like to call these thresholds, which often feel like crisis points, *initiations into authenticity.* They point toward new, urgent requirements of self-responsibility. Unfamiliar choices must be made. And this is the true opening into what the Greeks called *authentikos,* from which we get our English word *authenticity.*

One example illustrating an initiation into authenticity is a psychic shift that I've noticed we all experience between the ages of 28 and 30. This particular change emphasizes that each of us become deeply responsible for our lives as we mature. Even though modern society holds that we become adults between the ages of 18 and 21, in my experience that's simply not accurate.

What I've observed is that up until we're 21, we're in the business of meeting many of the fated components of our lives: aspects of our Cosmic Contracts that relate to personality development, family legacy, cultural influence, and other significant early events (including the ending of childhood and adolescence). By the time we're 21, we're far enough out of our teens to begin negotiating certain cultural expectations based on the previous formative years. Yet the adult ego is still developing, making it crucial that we work to discover who we are over the course of the next seven to eight years.

Then, around age 28, something happens—a threshold is reached, an initiation begins, a crisis occurs, and in some fundamental way we're confronted with all the unconscious ways that we've been creating our lives based on our history and the pressure of externally imposed expectations. This situation raises a fundamental question: *What parts of my ego structure are in allegiance to my past in ways that are now blocking my Destiny?* The answer we get will relate greatly to how we've been unconsciously fashioning our existence, like children blindly following the directives of our parents. Yet now a new level of growth is required, which demands that we begin to nurture and lead ourselves in order to keep growing into our Destiny.

Until our 30s, most of us were significantly identified with familial; civil (local government, political, and law enforcement); and positional (those holding status in society such as teachers, bosses, and religious delegates) authority. As such, we may have made many choices based on what others wanted for us—choices that weren't in harmony with who we really are or are meant to become.

Although this is a common initiation into authenticity that most of us experience when we enter our 30s, similar turning points can occur anytime in our lives to challenge superficial connections with our soul. Such transitions occur when the environment has directed our course in life, and in order to feel accepted, we've acquiesced to outer demands. Simply put, initiations into authenticity are given to us by the Universe to challenge the areas in our lives where other external forces choose for us the course our lives take.

Even what may appear to be an outer form of rebellion may be nothing more than succumbing to identification with the very outer authority that has oppressed us. I've found this to be quite common with those who hold a minority or marginalized status in our culture. For example, many individuals who are oppressed become exactly what the dominant group has labeled them as being—and then claim that as a form of liberation. African-American men, who are identified by society as potential troublemakers and criminals, may become gangbangers and claim that label as power. Gay men accused of being overly sexual beings become promiscuous, declaring that as liberation. Feminists who are seething with rage toward women who prefer to stay at home and raise kids repress other women's freedom to define their womanhood. In all of these cases, each group's reaction to the restrictive cultural label winds up exemplifying that very thing, and in doing so the members lose their capacity to choose otherwise.

To become authentic, it's imperative that we continually discern whether we're living harmoniously with our inner values. Are we simply mistaking conditioned responses—formed out of the unconscious patterning of our past—for what we really hold true? This discernment offers us the opportunity to develop something that's key to transforming Fate into Destiny via wielding our power of choice: *inner authority.*

Inner Authority

Through our initiations into authenticity, the need to develop inner authority comes to call—and we're challenged to stand for something based on our integrity. Inner authority is an internal orientation toward the outer world. It allows us to consciously manage collective and generational influences that would otherwise usurp our capacity to make soul-directed decisions.

Therefore, to develop greater input from our higher selves and true free will, the Universe issues each of us tasks at different points in our lives (and to the degree that we're ready) that challenge us to become more of what we really are. This often necessitates a trial of some kind in which the environment seems to conspire against us, challenging our authentic self to step up to the plate. Inevitably, it demands that we shed the components that made up our past identity—and this means a shift in the way the ego relates to authority found outside of ourselves.

Civil, cultural, positional, religious, and familial authorities aren't inherently negative. For example, parental power—a component of familial authority—is necessary as a guiding force in a child's development. But as we mature, our soul will demand a break from parental and, perhaps, cultural controls that block or undermine our becoming individuals. It's here that inner authority becomes a crucial key to transforming the Fate our past has given us into the Destiny of unlived potential. The lifetime task of developing inner authority, which is particularly emphasized as we enter our 30s, is essential to the fulfillment of our agreement with Destiny. It demands that we reap what we sow and take full responsibility for the person we are, have been, and want to become by making different decisions anchored by our soul.

We'll constantly measure parental and cultural values against our new emerging personal ones. Although much of our inheritance may resonate with our soul's purpose, whenever there's a chasm between that legacy and the calling of the soul, our psyches will enter into a state of chaos. A life crisis will ensue that's proportional to the gap between the outer world and our true selves. At this juncture, our inner authority lays the foundation of our authentic adult values, which we'll continually reference, develop, and evolve throughout our entire lives as we become more empowered and soulful.

The greater our inner authority, the more accessible the ego becomes to the soul as a creative vessel through which the authentic self can enter—and the more soulful we become. This gives rise to a healthy ego, a self-concept built upon your intrinsic connection to all of life, yet allows you to retain your own distinct identity as an individual. Through inner authority, a healthy ego has an inviolable, centered sense of where authentic power emanates from, which is the soul.

At this point, we're entering into the territory of self-esteem, but that's truly not enough for a healthy ego, because it's often based on transitory sociocultural definitions of power. In my experience, we need something called *soul-esteem.* It's our next key ingredient to consider in authentic choice making and transforming Fate into Destiny.

Soul-Esteem

Initially, we develop self-esteem in the way I define it—or its lack—based on feedback from our environment. That outer approval becomes the arbiter of how we feel about ourselves on any given day. This externalized support system for the ego fluxes as often as the fashions of a season—or the opinions of our friends.

It's easy to recognize what kind of esteem people rely upon. Those who mostly depend on self-esteem will often, for example, build it up by possessing something external that gives them a sense of value—such as having an expensive car, plastic surgery, or a certain brand of clothing. Esteem at this level is fragile. It comes and goes like the wind, and renders the ego weak, dependent primarily on outer approval.

Soul-esteem is not tied to the outer world and passing fads. It emanates from within—the eternal, intrinsic, and Divine part of our being that knows we have the same value as every being alive in this Universe. Soul-esteem empowers the ego to perceive our inherent Divine equality. It doesn't seek to divide and conquer others for a sense of being *better than;* it isn't competitive.

A healthy ego supported in this way makes us a transformational force within our culture, as opposed to its by-product. Soul-esteem pulls us out of judgment and allows us to perceive our faults and the flaws of others with compassion. We accept and love all that we see in each other, even though we may not *like* it. Soul-esteem doesn't depend on age, social status, or gender because it comes from our inner Buddha nature—our soul—which is detached from the temporal nature of life and exists without judgment like a tranquil and reflective lake within us.

Soul-esteem can't be instantly prayed into being; it takes time and must be sourced from within through continual effort, often requiring the discipline and honor code of a mystic. This development is forever a work in progress. We must always be mindful of when we're seeking and chasing outer approval for our value. For the degree to which we believe in our inherent worth determines how much we can change the world through our Destiny.

Soul-esteem is the foundation of inner authority, for without it, we don't possess ourselves—we are possessed by the world. We stand outside of our authenticity and our capacity to make conscious choice is greatly diminished. We're left vulnerable to becoming victims of cultural spells and what others believe we are.

But what exactly is a cultural spell, and how do we know if we're under one? Furthermore, how does that relate to making empowered choices and transforming Fate into Destiny?

Cultural Spells

In this age of all-pervasive media, it's enormously important to discern when we're being put under *cultural spells*. They're all around us, and their most obvious form is advertising. These enchantments are illusions cast by governments, politicians, religious organizations, special-interest groups, news organizations, commercial businesses, and various individuals. The spells are designed to hijack your power of choice by seducing your ego into getting its affirmation from something other than your soul. They're essentially designed to keep you from thinking for yourself and questioning authority. Here are some that are pervasive in our culture:

- Looking young for your age is important to remaining attractive and desirable.
- If you're a good person, good things will happen to you.
- You must have a college education to succeed at work.
- An abundance of money and respected social status are necessary for success.
- If you oppose a war, you're not in support of your country and its troops.
- You must be thin to be attractive.
- Women must be curvaceous and have large breasts to be beautiful.
- Men must be muscular to be handsome.
- Men should be masculine in temperament, and women should be feminine.

- You need someone else to complete you as your soul mate or "other half."
- Being white is better than having darker skin.
- You should never be satisfied with what you have, but always aspire to something more—even if it's not realistically attainable.
- You're entitled to be happy all the time.
- You need to buy the latest versions of consumer goods and keep up with trends.
- You should get what you want when you want it.
- There's only one definition of right and wrong.
- Being straight is better than being gay.
- The United States is the best country in the world.
- True love and intimacy are all about romance.
- If you're unhealthy, you must be doing something wrong and should fix it.
- The world is divided into winners and losers.

- Your religion is the only true one.
- One political party has all the answers to societal problems.

The degree to which you've developed soul-esteem and inner authority is the degree to which you're immune to the influence of these spells. Their power should never be underestimated. For example, it was a cultural spell set into motion by Adolf Hitler that generated the Holocaust.

Paradoxically, these enchantments can also be positive. Although some people in the media, such as Oprah Winfrey, use their spell-casting power to benefit humanity, we don't see nearly enough spells of love, kindness, generosity, and unity being created by the powers that be.

Whether positive or negative, however, these influences are often insidious. Most are generated out of consumerist agendas that seek to convince us that we need this or that product or service to be whole, valued, or accepted. How ironic that whenever we take action to *improve* ourselves based on these spells, we're activating a sense of not being good enough. We loop into our subconscious mind (the same part that hypnotherapists access to plant suggestions) that we're not okay as we already are, and this belief sabotages us.

For example, we lose weight only to gain it back again. Efforts to improve ourselves that derive from being under a cultural spell of not being good enough subconsciously reinforce that we're unworthy as we are. This makes our attempts to "fix" ourselves acts of self-violence. With the spell cast, we're hypnotized to believe that we need to be more, do more, have this, or have that in order to be *good enough*. We're fated to feel "less than" when in fact, as Buddhism teaches, we're already brilliant diamonds (soul-esteem). There's simply nothing to improve! Our real task is found in shedding the illusions of those destructive cultural spells that keep us from seeing our intrinsic value and embodying it. Therefore, in order to develop soul-esteem, we must direct all actions dealing with self-improvement toward the awakening of the good that's already present in us—and always has been. Cultural spells have the power to convince us that we're meant to be an apple when our soul's design is like that of an orange seed. When we're enchanted, we're fated to try to be something we're not.

Our inner authority determines how well we can withstand these projections onto our identity. Indeed, the spells we're under—and we're all subject to their influence—determine the degree to which we're able to claim our authentic power of choice and soul-direction. By discerning where we've been fooled into thinking that we originate in this temporal world (as opposed to being a soul incarnate within it), we can assess where our life's path has been hijacked by our environment and reestablish our soul coordinates here on Earth. This allows our inner authority to act like a Global Positioning System for the soul.

Here's an exercise that will help you assess the coordinates of your soul in relation to the cultural spells you may be under.

A Soul-Esteem Assessment of Your Cultural Spells

The following questions are designed to help you figure out where you're under cultural spells and to what degree. They also should assist you in investigating what you authentically value and how you embody that in the choices you make every day. Remember that to use your power of choice in transforming Fate into Destiny, you must be able to discern where a cultural spell is doing the choosing for you. Write down your initial responses in the journal I mentioned in Chapter 1, and then take a few days to see if you can identify on your own some other cultural spells you're under.

- Do you find yourself seduced by media hype and the latest trends?
- Do you feed off gossip and readily believe all you read in the tabloid headlines?
- Is it important to you to go to trendy restaurants or wear only designer labels? Do you worry about being considered cool, hip, or fashionable?
- How important is it to have the newest cell phone, iPod, car, or computer?
- Do you mimic the choices of all your friends? In a group, do you morph to fit those people's values and their ideas of who you are? Are you easily swayed by public opinion?

- What affirms your life and gives you a sense of personal value, fulfillment, beauty, and pleasure?

- How do you know that your values are truly your own rather than ones you inherited from your family or culture that aren't resonating with your inner core?

- How do you arrive at what you find attractive? How do you know that you're intrinsically attracted to it versus liking something because the media told you to?

- Do you allow your values to refine and shift with age, or do you think that they must stay the same—and be Botoxed into place? How do you try to keep your history alive and block the unfolding of your future?

- Do you believe in the cultural spell that aging is a bad thing? For example, do you think that you should idealize a wrinkle-free face in your 50s and 60s the way you did when you were in your 20s? How can this be applied to the rest of your life? What other values do you try to stabilize—to the detriment of your potential—because others say they're necessary to being accepted and considered beautiful?

- Are the choices you make in alignment with your values, or do they betray what you say is important, revealing deeper insecurities?

- What does your culture tell you about yourself that you believe to be true and that wounds your capacity to love yourself? Can you name this spell?

- What do you consider to be your worth? How much will you sell yourself for to get the approval of others? What can buy you?

- Do you believe everything that your government tells you to? How about religious authorities? How much do you question what you hear on the nightly news?

Make it a practice to spend ten minutes every day assessing your choices and self-regard. Who's really doing the choosing? Where is your self-worth coming from?

The Power of Authentic Choice: Nancy's Story

Nancy, a longtime client from Los Angeles, came to me after a major wake-up call that led her to ask herself some life-changing questions. Growing up in Beverly Hills with a famous mother, Nancy had a life carved out of cultural spells. Most of her days centered on wearing the latest fashions, eating at trendy restaurants, driving the newest car, and maintaining an A-list associate status in Hollywood's cult of celebrity. That was until Fate intervened and brought her world to a standstill via a plastic-surgery procedure that nearly took her life.

It was this Divine intervention that prompted her to seek me out. When I intuitively read her, I tracked a family legacy in which there was a concentrated focus on social persona such that her parents (most notably her mother) didn't know who they were—only what others thought of them. As Nancy matured, she was anchored by a set of Hollywood values, dictating that image was everything. Her mother trained her to be vigilant in managing her public persona, to be concerned about how others perceived her, and to mold herself into whatever the latest collective idea of glamour demanded.

I communicated my impressions to my client, who then told me about her recent visit with Fate. At age 40, having already undergone numerous plastic surgeries, Nancy felt compelled to get some light liposuction as a touch-up. She was slated to go to a premiere for a movie her husband had helped produce, and she wanted to be sure she'd meet the red-carpet standards of "Hollywood thin."

She was only under a local anesthetic, but she knew something had gone very wrong when she started to feel dizzy. She eventually lost consciousness; at that point, she briefly left her body and was met by her deceased father.

With love in his eyes, he asked, "Who are you, Nancy? Do you even know? Are you willing to die to be someone you're not?" Then he said, "The foundation of your life is built on a fault line. This is your first earthquake, and another is coming unless you rebuild your life out of the danger zone."

Then he kissed her and told her that it wasn't her time and that he'd see her again when it was. Nancy felt herself come back into her body, but she didn't regain consciousness until hours later. When she came to, she found herself surrounded by her family in the recovery room. She discovered that her body had reacted severely to the local anesthetic, which was strange because it hadn't happened in the numerous other surgeries she'd had. It was as if her body had decided that enough was enough. It seemed as though it was demanding a soulful capacity to honor it as it was, not as *others* thought it should be.

As I helped Nancy investigate and symbolically decode her experiences, I told her that living in Los Angeles meant she was indeed living on a fault line—both literally and symbolically. So many of our cultural spells are created and disseminated through Hollywood's media channels. It was my sense that for my client to get strong and truly heal, she'd need to move out of the city until she was strong enough to return with a new foundation, built on inner authority and soul-esteem.

I also knew that her current marriage wouldn't be able to contain this awakening, out of which the *new* Nancy was scheduled to emerge. Her life had been created out of cultural spells that did the choosing for her because she lacked an inner center. She'd inherited the pattern from both her parents, but the meeting with her father indicated that a new Destiny was at hand.

It's quite common for clients to contact me for a follow-up every year or so after our first consultation. At our next session, 12 months later, Nancy was irrevocably changed. She told me that for perhaps the first time in her life, she'd started making authentic choices supported by her soul. Her first decision was to leave her husband and move to Colorado. She decided to use the Fate of a near-death experience as a catalyst toward a new Destiny.

As of our last session, Nancy (now 44) hasn't had any more cosmetic surgery and has no plans to return to Los Angeles. When her mother passed away, she inherited a small fortune. She used it to found a center that asks plastic surgeons to donate their time and skills for children born with birth defects or who have been severely injured/burned. She told me that working with these patients has given her a sense of soul, and now she knows who she is. Eventually she got remarried to a doctor she met through the center. Having let go of a life of cultural spells, she transforms others' Fate into Destiny. She takes what Fate has given children with respect to birth defects or tragic accidents and helps them heal through it.

That's how it's done, folks!

Inner authority, supported by soul-esteem, is the fundamental key to activating your authentic power of choice. The degree to which it's developed is the degree to which you can consciously pick your direction and create a more life-affirming future. Otherwise, your history and culture will do the choosing for you. In this way, inner authority is the primary resource that must be developed when we want to engage in the authentic power of choice. And although authentic choice is a crucial instrument in transforming Fate into Destiny, it demands that we often next implement yet another tool.

Paradoxically, the most powerful choice we often have is that of *surrendering our power of choice.* Therefore, our next tool is indeed *the power of surrender.* In the next chapter, we'll look deeply at what *surrender* actually means—it's not necessarily what our Judeo-Christian culture has led us to believe.

Chapter 3

SURRENDER

"Remember the deep root of your being, the presence of your lord. Give your life to the one who already owns your breath and your moments. If you don't . . . you'll be wasting the treasure of your life and foolishly ignoring your dignity and your purpose."

— Rumi

The concept of surrender is found in most spiritual texts and traditions worldwide. It's often misinterpreted, used by many religious institutions to strip members of their personal power, leaving them bereft of a sense of self. For example, during medieval times, the papacy demanded that money, sexuality, property, and allegiance be *surrendered* to the church in order to earn salvation. This gave the Vatican enormous wealth and power, while leaving many individuals with nothing but vows of chastity and poverty. This isn't an authentic model of surrender—which isn't about relinquishing your power to another human being or institution—although it's what most of us in Western Judeo-Christian culture will reference when considering the subject.

Authentic surrender occurs when we release the ego as the center point of choice and let the soul decide. This is one of the most frightening and challenging choices we can make because it requires a loss of ego, yet it's the only option that assures we don't lose our souls. It allows human will to be merged with Divine design. The ego isn't necessarily concerned with the highest good, as it can only look out for our survival-based needs and fears. In addition, it often experiences a soul choice as a defeat. This is something we've all experienced and comes up quite often when a romantic or otherwise-significant relationship ends. My client Stacy is a good case in point.

Letting the Soul Decide

Stacy came to me for a reading because she was in the midst of a divorce from Scott, whom she'd been married to for three years. At the beginning of the relationship, she'd told him that she had no interest in having children. Scott stated that he shared the same values and wished to build a life solely with her. But two years into the marriage, he not only wanted kids, but he began to sabotage his wife's birth control.

Eventually Stacy became pregnant and discovered that her husband had been lying all along about his desire to have children. One of his best friends shared that Scott had always wanted kids but didn't tell her because he thought that she'd eventually come around to the idea. Realizing that this would never be the case, he'd taken matters into his own hands.

When Stacy became pregnant, Scott refused to agree to her getting an abortion—which she felt forced her to have one without telling him. Needless to say, the marriage ended with much acrimony. It was then that she came to me, seeking guidance about the divorce settlement.

When I intuitively read her, I realized that she was engaged in a battle between her ego—which wanted justice and vengeance for Scott's duplicitous actions—and her soul. This war was nothing new to Stacy. She'd lost friends, employees, and the support of family throughout her life because of her need to react and hurt others when she felt wronged. Due to the subterfuge regarding her birth control, she was considering suing Scott, in addition to financially destroying him through the divorce settlement.

I could sense that this situation was brought about so that my client could develop new pathways in her consciousness that would allow her soul more authority in the choices she made. The ego battle of divorce—which can be brutal if both spouses seek compensation for the wrongs they felt were done to them—was the perfect container to develop her much-needed power of surrender.

As the reading progressed, Stacy told me that she had to decide how much she wanted to sue Scott for to compensate for the pain and suffering the abortion had caused her. She wanted to know if I could intuit the outcome and give her some advice. But I challenged her, letting her know that this wasn't really what had brought her to me.

"Tell me, Stacy," I began, "regarding your divorce settlement, what would your soul decide?" For a moment she tried to answer but couldn't even speak. Then I watched as her previous venomous ranting transformed into a river of tears. My question had released her ego's alignment with her inner victim. She knew that her soul would decide to forgive Scott, seek an equitable divorce settlement without litigation, and let go of the betrayal so that she could truly move on. Pursuing this situation was the perfect mirror for her to see the ways in which she'd unconsciously betrayed her authentic honor code many times in her life. Her higher self knew that Scott simply had a contract to be her teacher.

The soul doesn't seek revenge, recompense, or validation—it knows its Divine worth. Still, its choices will baffle the ego time and time again because the soul sees the Divine in all beings and events—even in the natural disaster, car accident, murderer, prostitute, rapist, child abuser, and pedophile. Yes, this list will push some buttons in you. It does in me, too, but we must embrace the saying *God doesn't make bad people; people do bad things.* Either All is One, or All is not One; either All is of God, or All is not of God. This is one truth that we can't just turn off when it's inconvenient for the biases of the ego. In times of testing, Christians are often asked to consider, *What would Jesus do in this situation?* That's another way of asking, *What would the soul choose?*

Christ's crucifixion was baffling to his followers—and to Pontius Pilate—who didn't understand why Jesus didn't save himself. As Jesus hung on the cross and birthed the archetype of crucifixion, he was symbolically communicating that each of us will one day suffer on a cross in our own lives when we experience the crucifixion of our ego's allegiance to survival reality and negative forms of outer authority that compete with the voice of our soul.

It's as if Jesus were saying, symbolically, *Hey, humanity, this is how you let the soul decide. You must surrender the ego to the authority of the soul. Release your loyalty to the fear of death and the approval of others. Death is not the end, but a transition to a greater consciousness—that of the soul. Watch me. This is how you, too, can incarnate your soul; this is the way it's done. This is how you can transform Fate into Destiny.*

Where Do You Need to Let Your Soul Decide?

Take a moment and allow yourself to reflect on where you aren't letting your soul decide something in your life. Where are you holding on and seeking revenge, validation, or the fulfillment of your ego's need for payback? Be sure to write your answers down in your journal and reflect on them as you progress through this book.

The time comes in all of our lives when we're given the opportunity to let the soul decide. But in order to do so, we must first surrender our ego and its illusory sense of victim entitlement. As soon as you hear yourself say that something isn't fair, make a note that your inner victim is speaking, because only that part of you sees life that way. For your ascension to occur out of the crucifixion, relinquish the idea that anything is fair or unfair, and let the soul take it from there. This is true surrender of the magnitude that can transform Fate into Destiny, restore the Garden of Eden, and make Heaven a place on Earth.

If we stay focused on life's crucifixions, we'll never experience what really matters—the true point of being here! Only the power of surrender can help us achieve this. Then we're aligned with the next tool in transforming Fate into Destiny: *the power of prayer.*

Chapter 4

PRAYER

Prayer is a supremely powerful tool, yet I believe that we need an updated and clarified understanding about what it actually is and how it works. Many folks relate to prayer solely as something repetitious that's said at a Catholic mass or while holding a rosary. While I respect chanting and other repetitious mantras, when I'm speaking about prayer, I'm referring to establishing a conscious dialogue with God, the Universe, your soul, life force itself, and much more.

In her beautiful book *Illuminata: A Return to Prayer,* author Marianne Williamson has this to say about prayer:

> Prayers increase our faith in the power of good and thus our power to invoke it. Most of us have more faith in the power of AIDS to kill us than we have faith in God to heal us and make us whole. We have more faith in the power of violence to destroy us than we

> have faith in the power of love to restore us. Where we place our faith, there we will find our treasure. Whatever we choose to look at, we will see. Prayer is a way of focusing our eyes.

Prayers are requests we make of our Higher Power to align us with a different force field, a new center of gravity and power source. This allows us to release our subconscious mind's allegiance to our ego and the messages of the outer world that are programming it so that it can be infused with Divine inner guidance for our lives. One prayer can allow heaven to intervene and vibrationally shift your energy, aligning you with your soul's intention and highest potential in any circumstance.

But what *is* prayer if it's not solely repetitively chanting? What is this tool that triggers events to unfold for the highest good of all via a transmission of grace? Prayer can be many things: visualizing God sending light to surround and heal someone going through a difficult circumstance; speaking to God about the day; requesting strength, courage, or patience to endure a difficult time; asking the Universe to give you guidance in any situation; lighting a candle in a church on behalf of someone else; and much more. Essentially, it can be any request for Divine intervention in any circumstance; it can also be an offering made to the Earth.

Prayer has many forms that often serve as vehicles for dialogue with a Higher Power and as ritualized ways to channel the Divine into our lives and those of others. However, one thing stands out clearly to me from my years of service as an intuitive: *The prayers we say and what we ask for through them reveal an awful lot about how we perceive reality, what we value, and what gives us meaning on the journey of life*. Think about that for a minute.

What kind of spiritual conversations do you have? What do they reveal about your reality?

By exploring these questions, I've realized that our communication generally falls into two categories: *ego prayers* and *soul prayers*. Let's look at each of them closely because I've found that the latter have the power to transform Fate into Destiny, while the former often get a negative response from heaven.

Ego Prayers vs. Soul Prayers

We've all said an ego prayer before—I know I have (and still do!). These are often based out of what we *want,* not what we *need;* and they rarely have the best interests of others at heart. Let's review an ego prayer to help you identify when you're saying one (oh, and let's also look at "God's" response!).

> *Dear God,*
>
> *It's Mike here. I usually don't ask for much, but I'd really like my new Internet business selling children's toys to take off so I can quit my job. I hate my current boss. He's always criticizing me and never appreciates the hard work I do—he totally reminds me of my father!*
>
> *This new book I'm reading says that prayer and visualization are powerful, so I'm going to visualize making a million dollars by next year through this new Internet gig—could you give me a hand with that? It would be great if you could help me manifest it! Then I could quit my current job, get some cool clothes, buy a house, lease a new BMW, and have*

money to travel to the Bahamas next fall. I could finally ask my girlfriend, Jane, to marry me.

On that note, it would also be great if you could help Jane. I do love her, but sometimes she's so stubborn. I sure wish she'd change that about herself and quit fighting with me about having kids. I know she says that she doesn't want children, but I really want to start a family. If you help me make that million, then she won't have to work and might be persuaded to stay at home and raise kids.

Oh, if you grant me these things, I promise I'll give 10 percent of my income to charity and be sure to give some money to each homeless person I see.

Please let me know your answer by this Friday—please give me an unmistakable sign!

Thanks, God.
Mike

God's answer:

My dear Mike,

In short, the answer to all your requests is no. So when nothing remarkable has happened by Friday, take note that I have turned you down. Although you cannot remember it right now, before you came to Earth you made certain agreements that must be upheld, and answering your prayer would violate many of those agreements.

Let me give you a glimpse of things from my perspective: First of all, before you were born, you made an agreement with your boss that he would come into your life at this time to help you heal your issues with your father and how his criticism wounded you. This means that your boss must treat you much like your dad did in order to trigger your old wounds so that they surface again and can be dealt with now that you are an adult. There is a deep lesson here that you must learn. Your boss is your teacher, and until you learn what you need to and heal, you cannot move on to the next stage of your life.

This is very important to accept, because where you are going next with your life will require that you learn how to validate yourself in ways your father could not. You are going to be running a major company in the years to come and will need to be a true leader with authentic soul-esteem. Since that is not done yet, you need to stay in the same job.

Second, you will soon be informed that the toys you are thinking of selling are toxic due to a chemical in the plastic. Be grateful, my dear Mike, that you will not be able to get the business off the ground. To that end, I am setting it up so that your girlfriend will "accidentally" unleash a computer virus, crashing your system for two weeks while news of the toys gets to you. This will save you from harming children, from being sued, and from enduring much grief. Yes, you will be mad at Me, but take care . . . you cannot see what I can.

Now about this financial request—you are not yet mature enough to handle a million dollars, and you certainly are not going to give 10 percent of it to charity! That amount of cash would exploit current flaws in your character that you are not aware of and hinder your spiritual development. At this point, you are not able to manage the choices that come with that much money.

Your current car works just fine, by the way. I will make sure it continues to since you do need it to get to work. I will also ensure that you have enough money to fulfill all your needs—but not your wants. Let's look at more of those: Although you do not know it yet, in two years you will be moving from Milwaukee to Chicago for an incredible job, so it is not wise to buy a house now that you will have to sell in two years. The market will be bad then. Oh, and there is going to be a major hurricane hitting the Bahamas next fall that would have taken your life, so it is a good thing that you will not have the money to go there.

As far as Jane goes, she is there to teach you to accept others as they are—and to never pray for them to change. She is not meant to have children in this lifetime and will soon discover that she is actually not able to. She is not the right person for you to commit to in marriage, and once you accept her as she is, you will know that. You have a contract to meet someone in three years who is going to want to have a family with you, so once again it's a good thing that you do not have enough money for a wedding.

Mike, I know you cannot see all of this through your egocentric point of view, but do not worry—I have your back.

Love,
God

P.S. You should already be giving the homeless a dollar and a prayer as a way of affirming your connection to Me. They are as much a part of Me as you are.

Ego prayers originate mainly out of what we *think* we want and need. As we discovered with cultural spells, sometimes these are things we're told are important by the media and our culture, parents, and peers. As we look at Mike's prayer, so much of what he's longing for comes from his ego's small perspective. He can't see the larger design of his life and how future events are going to unfold.

Although every prayer we say is answered without exception—whether positively or negatively—I sense that the ones originating in our egos might make the Divine laugh! And they often aren't effective in transforming the Fate of a circumstance into Destiny.

Now in contrast with this, let's look at a soul prayer.

> *Dear God,*
>
> *It's Victoria here. All of my previous requests to be a breakout success as a fashion photographer here in New York City seem to have been ignored. I'm having a really hard time in my life right now; my heart is very heavy. I know I'm meant to be learning things, and with Your grace, I can get through this period.*
>
> *You know that I'm currently in a job I can't stand. I hate waiting tables when I have a master's degree in art and photography—it's so humiliating. I feel like such a failure. How am I going to continue to get by as a waitress living here in New York? Although I came here two years ago to explore creative opportunities in the fashion industry, nothing is panning out, and I feel lost and invisible. Am I on the right path? Is there another way I'm meant to use my talents and skills? Waiting tables can't be all there is for me in this lifetime—right?*

Please show me what I need to learn so that I can go on to the next part of my journey. I'm willing to look at whatever I need to within myself in order to heal and move my life forward.

Although I thought I wanted to be in the fashion world, now I'm not so sure. On the few photo shoots I've worked on, I've realized it's not all it seems to be. But I want to be of creative service to others and to capture their essence on film. I just don't know what to do since nothing seems to sustain me here professionally. As You know, I didn't land that last job I was up for as an assistant photographer for Vogue.

What's more, money has been really tight. Christmas is coming up, and I really need to see my family—please help me find a way. Right now I can't afford it because they live in Idaho, and it's hard to get a cheap ticket there. I'm already picking up extra shifts to make more money. I miss them so much, so if You could help me out, I'd really appreciate it. I need to be surrounded by something real for a while; I feel like I need to get my soul back.

And then there's Steve, my boyfriend of the last year. I know I met him for a reason, but please help me understand why I feel so insecure in our relationship. What lesson does he have to teach me about myself? Please help us discover if we're meant to move further in our commitment to each other. I know You're guiding us, and I hope that if I'm not the right one for him in the long term, You'll bless him with someone who is.

I'd really like my life in New York to begin to flourish; it's been hard these past two years. But if You want me somewhere else, I'm ready to accept that now. Show me what my soul came here to do. I'm hanging by a thread. Please use me in whatever way You'd like. I am Yours.

Humbly,
Victoria

God's answer:

Dear Victoria,

It is so good to receive such a soulful prayer from you. I have been waiting for you to say this for two years. I know that you have been having a hard time and things have been tough, but it has all led you to this point of authentic surrender.

Although you came to New York City wanting to be a fashion photographer, that is not really your dream, but only what you thought you wanted in order to belong and "be somebody." Things have not worked out over the past two years so that you would begin to clarify what your soul truly wants to create this lifetime.

You are just about done with this lesson, my dear. I will sustain you through this time of difficulty as your ego's desires burn out and your heart ignites. You were never meant to work in the world of fashion, and you wouldn't have been truly happy there. But you are indeed meant to be a professional photographer. When you are finally ready, I am going to help you become incredibly successful.

For now, you must learn the lesson of humility and surrender. When you can feel just as good about yourself as a waitress as you would being a famous photographer, then you will be ready for the next steps in your journey. Until then, you must stay in your current job.

Listen to your intuition and inner self, Victoria, for I am always speaking to you. In two weeks, right before Christmas, a wealthy man is going to come to the restaurant where you work. He will challenge you with his dismissive attitude, testing your humility. If you do not match his elitist energy, you will be shocked to find that he tips you $1,000 and you have enough money to go home and see your family. I will send you many signs and support to ensure that you succeed.

During your stay at home, you will feel inspired and compelled to take pictures of the beautiful snow-covered landscape in Idaho. When you get back to New York City and develop the photos, Steve will tell you (with tears in his eyes) that your photos are amazing and have really captured the soul of your home. This is to help you see where your true talent lies, and you will feel an internal shift in that very moment.

This is your soul remembering its agreement with Destiny to take photos around the world that will help everyone who moves to New York City and struggles as you have to remember what matters. Part of your purpose is to remind others of the places they call home when they feel that they are lost.

That is, in part, your true calling—your soul's Destiny. And once you figure that out, your life will take off in many directions while your photos are showcased in galleries all over the city. Steve really does love you, by the way, and you are meant to learn how to accept that gift without doubting it or feeling insecure because you do not believe that you are worthy. Once you realize more of your true worth, your commitment with him will deepen into spiritual partnership.

In spite of outer appearances, all is well, Victoria. And I will speak to you through your dreams tonight so that when you wake up in the morning, you will just know inside that everything is working out for your highest good because you have surrendered your life to Me—and have thus aligned your ego with your soul. You will wake up knowing that I have answered most of your prayers affirmatively.

Yours truly,
God

Soul prayers come from a humble place within us. We're able to speak with God this way when we realize that we're small in this vast cosmos, but we matter to each other and to the Divine. In fact, most soul prayers involve an element of surrender, humility, and a wish to be of greater service to life. Throughout her heartfelt book *Invisible Acts of Power,* Caroline Myss explores the nature of soul prayers as they relate to our calling to be of service to each other. To that end, she writes this prayer:

May I be open and present to all guidance that directs me to be of spiritual support to others. And when I am in need of support, please direct me to those who You would select on my behalf. I remain forever grateful that You so closely and lovingly keep a mindful eye on all of us who share life on this earth. So often we do not understand why we must endure what is asked of us; in those times, grant me the grace of faith. May I always be guided to live a life of service that benefits humanity and the quality of my own spiritual journey.

Soul prayers animate the goodness of others and are the true medium for miracles. And although they can also arise out of our own personal authentic needs—which must be met to support actualizing our Destiny—these petitions don't aim to change anyone or make someone love us. Rather, they most often seek to channel grace for the highest good of all concerned and those who are connected to our requests. They take into account how small our ego's perspective can often be.

Soul prayers ask of the Divine: *Please infuse my contribution to this situation with your deepest wisdom and my highest potential. Show me, dear Universe, where I am afraid to hear Your answer to my prayer, where I am blocking my own clarity, and why.*

Writing a Prayer in Your Journal

To apply what you've just learned from this section on prayer, take a moment and write down in your journal a prayer to your understanding of the Divine. Don't think too much about what you're saying; just put out there to the Universe what you feel requires heavenly intervention.

Then go back and reread what you wrote to discern what parts of it are more ego driven, rather than directed by the soul. Next, rewrite it while consciously focusing on making it a soul prayer using my example and definition. Keep revising it until you are certain you've eliminated the ego.

Offer it up to the Divine, knowing that it has been answered. Assume that all that happens from this point forward is part of that response. Keep a daily record of how the reply comes to you, while remaining open to however it arrives. This is a wonderful way to use the power of prayer in transforming your Fate into Destiny.

Prayer is a conscious way to invoke the Divine as a co-creator in your life, as a request of assistance and grace. Yet we're each capable of holding the space of positive thought and intention ourselves as the other half of the co-creative process. This brings us to our final tool in transforming Fate into Destiny: *the Law of Attraction.*

Chapter 5

THE LAW OF ATTRACTION

Prayer is an invocation of the Divine to co-create with you—through the delivery of grace—into every circumstance on behalf of the highest good of each situation. On the other hand, *the Law of Attraction* is where we become responsible for aligning our own thoughts and intentions with positive energy and outcomes—where we create our own grace.

The Law of Attraction is a universal principle that posits: Like energy attracts like energy in this universe. And as we're all essentially energetic beings, your personal vibratory frequency (which is a by-product of what you do, focus on, believe, and think about) will attract to you people, situations, events, and opportunities that are a match.

In one of their books presenting the Teachings of Abraham, *The Amazing Power of Deliberate Intent,* Esther and Jerry Hicks say this about the Law of Attraction:

> In the same way that the law of gravity consistently responds to all of the physical matter of your planet, the *Law of Attraction* consistently responds to all vibrations. Every projection of thought, whether you are focused into the past, present, or future, is vibration and has attraction power. Each thought offers a signal, similar to a radio signal, that the *Law of Attraction* recognizes and matches. This powerful, consistent *Law of Attraction (that which is like unto itself is drawn)* offers consistent results in response to the vibrations that you offer.

The Law of Attraction is about consciously aligning ourselves vibrationally to thoughts and intentions that carry frequencies that hold the most affirming creative potential in any circumstance. To use the Law of Attraction, we must learn to manage our thoughts, engaging the imagination, and master our perception of reality. Essentially we learn that what we focus on is empowered and animated, attracting to us a quality of energy and informing how we experience events.

The power of this principle can't be denied. How many times do you wake up in a bad mood that you can't shake off? The next thing you know, your day just keeps getting worse as you draw to yourself one accident and frustrating scenario after another! And how many times do you wake up with a smile on your face only to be greeted by the smiles of others and positive happenstance at each turn of the day?

That said, because I've noticed that we must embrace this law in a more mature way, I must stress something crucial here about this phenomenon as it relates to your agreement with Fate. *The Law of Attraction can only be effective, both in positive and negative ways, within certain boundaries of your agreements with Fate and Destiny. Therefore it has limits of operation within your life's purpose, and can only transform Fate into Destiny when it's connected to the intentions of your soul and the Divine.*

In other words, the Law of Attraction is a creative power of the soul and simply can't be used to acquire what the ego wants if the soul isn't on board, for better or worse. Positively, however, the law can only magnetize the greatest potential that your life was designed to hold according to your purpose. It brings to you no more than what can be contained within the fated limits put in place to support your Destiny.

That said, I hope you can begin to grasp the enormous importance of dialoguing with your soul to ascertain the blueprint, plan, and Fate this part of you agreed to as a *Divinely* designed boundary—within which the Law of Attraction can magnetize your Destiny.

For example, many people in workshops have approached me and said, "Robert, I'm using the Law of Attraction, and still I can't seem to get what *I* [ego] want. What am I doing wrong? Am I 'counter-intending' what I'm trying to manifest?"

I've often given them a quick intuitive once-over and have had to disclose that they're pursuing the manifestation of something that wasn't intended for them in this lifetime. Rather, their ego, often driven by a cultural spell, wants something the soul isn't committed to—and if the soul isn't on board, the Law of Attraction can't blow wind into their sails and move the boat of their lives forward toward the next shore.

In addition, I've also been asked, "If I can't stop focusing on my desire to see harm come to someone I'm angry with, will that attract disaster to them or to me?"

To which I've often replied, "You're not quite so powerful that you can change the course of someone's life negatively simply because you're mad at them, and your Cosmic Contract demands otherwise." Can we send funky negative vibes—or constructive positive ones—to others, and does that have an effect on them? Absolutely! But luckily there are certain fated safeguards that protect us when it comes to how we can use the Law of Attraction to achieve what seem to be positive and negative ends. We must leave the major interventions up to God and the power of prayer.

Western Capitalism and Misinterpreting Abundance

To grasp how we can truly use this wonderful universal law of creation, we must make a much-needed cultural assessment of how we're interpreting it through our Western mind-set. Many spiritual teachers and motivational speakers today stress the importance of using this principle through positive thinking, visualization, and affirmations to manifest abundance. Unfortunately, though, I've noticed that quite often the focus is on attracting more *stuff.* Consequently, many people begin visualizing financial wealth, new cars, homes, soul mates, and the healing of illnesses (often believed to be exclusively the result of negatively mismanaging their thoughts). To be sure, what we focus on is expanded, and certain disorders *can* be aided (and often healed) by positivism.

But what about the illness that's a necessity for the soul's awakening? What about the creative depression that must be experienced as an initiation into the unlived life inside of us? What about the financial straits that must be endured in order to squeeze choice out of our lives, not allowing us to choose out of the ego's pride—ensuring that the soul's journey is kept on course?

Can the Law of Attraction take away these *necessary* situations intended to grow our soul? Does visualizing and acting *as if* these situations of *necessity* have been transformed always *objectively* change them? Does simply deciding to *see* them differently make them go away? No. Sometimes they're there for a very important reason (per our Fate) that's integral to our Destiny and must be accepted as such. But we can decide to see them as part of a greater purpose and not lose our power to them.

There's a difference between the denial of reality—such as having $100 in your bank account, although you keep visualizing $1 million and acting *as if* it's there, while nothing changes—and reorienting toward events and experiences as affirming and meaningful. The latter allows you to empower yourself to co-create reality through your *inner response* to them.

In other words, although you may want $1 million, maybe you're simply not meant to have it in this lifetime—but you can still see your life as *abundant,* regardless of your outer wealth. Choosing to see every situation as being infused with meaning, guidance, and grace is how the Law of Attraction is really meant to be applied. This means that the best way to access this fantastic principle is through *an attitude of gratitude.* In this way, the law is always effective in activating the highest potential of your life and will bring the greatest abundance it's designed to hold. Yet this prosperity means nothing if it's not transformed into service that gives back to humanity.

The Law of Attraction is more about our mental focus as it relates to the management of our personal power and less about getting more stuff. Furthermore, sometimes difficult things happen to us for reasons that have nothing to do with "thinking negative thoughts." Nonetheless, we do get to decide if we want to focus on the positive or negative of each situation, which will either empower or disempower us accordingly.

Because using the Law of Attraction means that we become responsible for the ways we choose to see events, it's one of the most powerful tools we have in transforming Fate into Destiny. It can be used to energize the gifts inherent within our Fate, based on what we choose to focus on—making each challenge an opportunity to bring forth the best of who we are and can be. Let me share with you another client story in which the Law of Attraction became a key in transforming Fate into Destiny, but also showed its limitations.

Amanda, Steven, and Blake: Attracting What's Real

Many years ago, Amanda contacted me for a reading when she was six months pregnant. She'd recently found out that her soon-to-be-born son, Blake, had Down syndrome. This would most likely result in birth defects that would require numerous surgeries, as well as some degree of possible mental retardation and cognitive issues. I'll never forget this reading, as I felt overwhelmed by a powerful presence around me before the session.

A longtime student of metaphysics, Amanda had been a practitioner of the Law of Attraction for many years and was quite devout. She claimed that her use of this principle had brought her many wonderful things, including her husband, her house, the job of her dreams, and three other beautiful children. Yet with the news of her unborn son's condition, her law-of-attraction bubble had burst and her reality was in crisis. She told me that she couldn't imagine how she could have attracted this situation to herself.

As I read Amanda, I knew that the strong presence I felt around me was Blake's soul. I sensed that he'd chosen the Fate of Down syndrome to teach others what was *real.* I knew that this couldn't be changed and that he'd come to open his mother's heart to the suffering of others—something she was out of touch with in her blessed life. In fact, she told me that she actually felt the need to block out the pain of other people so that it wouldn't contaminate her energy and positive focus!

Nonetheless, Blake had the energy of a master teacher and had a Cosmic Contract of teaching his parents and others the power of compassion. In fact, his energy was so strongly present during the session that I felt as if my heart would burst as I fought back tears, choking up while I communicated to Amanda what I was intuiting about her son. I was blown away by the caring and power of his soul to take on such a difficult contract and felt humbled in his presence.

Unfortunately, Amanda didn't take my news too well because it didn't fit into her law-of-attraction ideology. In fact, she told me that she was going to keep visualizing Blake as being born free of birth defects and completely healthy. As we ended the session, I left her with a prayer and said good-bye to Blake's soul. I thought I'd never hear from her again.

Then almost two years later, Amanda contacted me for a reading for both her and her husband, Steven. As

I'd previously sensed, although Blake seemed to be cognitively okay, he was indeed born with various physical problems and had already undergone numerous surgeries. Amanda told me that she felt like a failure because she was unable to manifest a healthy body for Blake using the Law of Attraction and visualization. She and her husband had recently separated, and he was also having trouble dealing with Blake's condition, but for other reasons.

I sensed that Steven was running from the situation because his son mirrored back to him his own wounds from childhood. As I read him, I kept getting the impression that he grew up feeling "deformed" himself. Steven later let me know that he grew up with a father who was very verbally abusive and critical, and that he never felt good enough. He said that he always felt like "damaged goods," and now he had a son who mirrored back his own deep wounds.

As the reading progressed, I could tell that Amanda still hadn't accepted the limitations in front of her. She'd internalized a sense of guilt, as if she'd failed her son because she couldn't use the Law of Attraction to get what her ego wanted. I also realized that Steven hadn't made the symbolic connection about why Blake had come into his life—as a way to heal his own inner sense of deformity. He couldn't love his son as is because he couldn't love himself. Neither of them was on board with their souls' contracts or the little boy's soul agenda.

I finally said to them, "Both of you have contracts with your son to grow into a more mature understanding of life. Blake is a powerful soul who, through his love for you both, chose the Fate of a deformed body to teach you something very important about the nature of the soul and life. If you keep fighting this contract, you'll never be able to reengage with the Law of Attraction positively again. Why don't you both make a list of the positives that Blake has brought into your lives—just as he is—and see how that works for you?"

They were speechless, but I'd finally gotten through to them, and they agreed to give it a shot. And let me tell you, the Law of Attraction kicked some ass! Within three months, Amanda contacted me and said that their family life had done a complete turnaround since that session and she finally got it. She understood that there was a Divine design at work and that Blake's condition was indeed a gift. She said, "Robert, each day I find more miracles and hidden blessings within this situation. I look at Blake and all I see is beauty, just as he his. I realize now how dogmatic I'd become about the Law of Attraction—so much so that I forgot that it's really just about gratitude for being alive."

Steven and Amanda were living together again and their marriage had never been better. Amanda told me that her husband was healing his childhood wounds through counseling. Around Christmas that year, I received a card with a picture of Steven, Amanda, their three other children, and Blake right in the center of the photo. He sparkled like a star.

After witnessing Amanda and Steven transform Blake's Fate into Destiny using the Law of Attraction, I realized that this principle is one of the most powerful tools we can use in transforming our Fate into Destiny. But first we must be willing to look our Fate in the eyes and greet it! When we do so, then we can energize the gifts inherent (the Destiny) within our Fate. And although we may want a limitless life regarding our desire for earthly things—whether it's financial wealth, a new house, a new car, to be married, or a healthy baby, in my experience it's best to first ask the soul/the Divine what's possible with our life's design. Surely you've heard of the saying, "Want to know how to make God laugh? Tell Him your plans!"

Don't get me wrong—I'm all for going after the best life you can have on all levels, including earthly abundance. (Bring it on—you know what I'm sayin'?) But when we try to be, have, or create something that our soul isn't in harmony with, we then fate ourselves to the exact opposite: an unfulfilled life, a path of suffering.

The Law of Attraction is intended to enhance your purpose and the soul's Cosmic Contact, not negate it. I must admit that it's quite tempting to adopt this law as yet another defense against our necessary, purposeful limits and mortal suffering; but to do so is not only ineffective, it does a great disservice to our capacity for compassion for one another and our humanity.

Chapter 6

PUTTING THE TOOLS TO WORK: A PERSONAL STORY

I'd like to share a personal story with you that demonstrates how I used the tools ***acceptance, authentic choice, surrender, prayer, and the Law of Attraction*** to transform a very fated cycle of my life into Destiny. During this time, which encompassed nearly two years of my life, I intuitively knew that I was going through a training period on how to use each tool. It felt like spiritual boot camp here on Earth!

To help you identify how I used these tools throughout this adventure, I have written the terms in bold italics where they appeared. There are some things mentioned in this story that I swore I'd never tell anyone, and yet here they are in print! I hope it serves you well.

Fate . . .

This story begins when I was 24 and had been living

in Seattle for nine months, struggling as an upstart intuitive-astrologer. I was having a rough ride both financially and emotionally—it was so bad that I must have been emitting an SOS signal to everyone who crossed my path. I said a ***prayer*** to the Universe to be shown what I needed to do in order to get out of my particular situation. My ego was hoping that the response would take shape as a mass of clients turning up, but God had another plan. Eventually, my answer showed up in the form of a stranger who tuned in to my distress signal and then gifted me with a significant message that started me on a new path.

One day I was working on a client's birth chart in a café when a man sat next to me and asked me if I was an astrologer. I told him that I was, and sensing my comfort level, he then confided to me that he was a professional psychic *and* astrologer. Having picked up on my general angst, he asked if I'd like to meet with him for coffee another day so that we could swap birth charts and give readings to each other. My intuition worked just fine for everyone else, but for my own life the signals seemed jammed and I couldn't get a clear read on anything. So I thought, *Why not? I've got nothing to lose. An objective point of view would be good for me. Let's see what he has to say.*

We met the next week at the same café, exchanged charts, and while he looked at mine, he asked, "Have you ever considered becoming a flight attendant?"

I just about knocked over my coffee and thought, *You've got to be kidding me. Are you smoking crack?!* Needless to say, my curt response was a bit dismissive. "Hell no," I replied. At the time, nothing about that job appealed to me.

But my new acquaintance adamantly explained to me that flight attendants typically only worked 12 days a month, and he pointed out that this kind of schedule would give me the time off to pursue my budding career as an intuitive-astrologer while having a base income. I'd received the guidance I'd asked for, but I didn't like it because it didn't fit in with my ego's plans. I left the café confused and frustrated.

A few weeks later, my life began to further unravel to the point that I was literally homeless. I was desperate and figured that what the man had suggested was the best guidance I'd gotten. So I made a new ***choice to surrender,*** and began the application process with a few airlines. I speak French fluently, so I thought with that asset and my likable personality, I'd be a shoo-in! Well, the Universe had other plans.

I interviewed with two major airlines and neither wanted me. I realized that I'd done some things wrong during the meetings, based on what they were looking for, and eventually I slipped into a deep depression and entered a very dark space. As my life in Seattle continued to sink like the *Titanic,* I was eventually forced to move back to Minneapolis (where I'd lived for seven years prior to Seattle). There I found refuge with my friend Cara in her new condo, which happened to have a spare guest room. I was also lucky enough to get back my old job, working with Cara at a hospital as an equipment dispatcher to patient-care units.

As I licked my wounds, I began to put the pieces of my life back together and gathered strength. In spite of the fact that I wasn't hired by two prominent airlines, I couldn't let go of this flight-attendant idea—in my heart, I knew it was authentic guidance from the Divine.

Eventually, I regrouped. With a fresh perspective, ready to animate the ***Law of Attraction*** with interview experience under my belt, I met with another major airline. I made it to a second interview, and afterward I ***prayed*** to the Universe that I'd be given the job. I used the ***Law of Attraction*** and visualized receiving it. I felt the happiness running through my body. I was grateful in advance for the forthcoming outcome (and although the true use of the ***Law of Attraction*** necessitates finding gratitude for *any* result that's in harmony with the greater good and plan for one's life, I *solely* visualized getting the position!). And yet I still received a rejection letter two weeks after the second interview.

The day that notice came, my heart broke, and I cried a bit. Once again, I felt abandoned by God, and I sank into a depression. I couldn't understand why I wasn't being hired! What did the Universe want me to do?

A few days later, I felt better, and although I couldn't articulate it at the time, in my heart I knew that I was being taught an extremely important life lesson about the nature of creation. So I made a ***choice*** to just ***accept*** that it wasn't meant to be. Once again, without knowing why events were unfolding the way they were, I ***surrendered*** to God. That night I had a dream in which I saw this beautiful gold-topped church. It was a powerful dream, and I knew that somehow it was guidance for me regarding my desire to be a flight attendant.

A week later, it was a beautiful summer day and I went for a jog around Lake Calhoun (a beautiful lake near downtown Minneapolis). As I was running, I was about halfway around the path when I looked toward the other side of the lake—and there I saw a beautiful gold-topped church. It was indeed the place from my dream. I stopped and wondered, *Am I going to meet someone important soon? Should I go to the church? What does this mean?*

Nothing of any importance whatsoever happened that day, and I didn't really feel compelled to go to the church, so I let it go and ***prayed*** to the Universe that I'd be shown what this all meant when the time was right (a ***soul prayer,*** I might add). The next day, one of my old fraternity brothers introduced me to a man who worked for American Airlines as a flight attendant—the one airline I had yet to interview with. This man told me that his employer was hiring and I should apply. As soon as I got home, I called their job hotline and requested an application. Once it arrived, I filled it out and sent it in right away. Nothing could have prepared me for what happened next.

A few days later, on October 1, 1997, I woke up feeling awful—not physically sick, but psychically overwhelmed. Something very difficult was coming my way—I could feel it. And although I was supposed to help some good friends move that day, I just couldn't get myself out of bed. I felt exhausted and depressed. Eventually I had to go to work, so I pulled myself together and drove to the hospital. Cara was working that day, too. She could tell that something was really wrong with me and asked what was up, but I couldn't articulate why I felt so bad. Hours later I received a phone call from my mother—one I will never forget. Having regressed into alcoholism, my father had committed suicide that morning. My heart shattered, and I felt angry and devastated.

Death brings forth a reality rupture that's often difficult to integrate and understand, and this was indeed a harsh truth to absorb, especially given the nature of my father's passing. Just days later, as I struggled to ***accept*** his choice to end his life, a representative from American Airlines called and asked if I could fly down to Dallas for an interview. I had an aunt in Fort Worth who couldn't make it to the funeral, and I thought it would be good to get out of the chaos for a bit and see her. Hopefully I'd be graced with a job that could allow my Destiny to take a new direction and bring some light to this dark time.

(As an aside, I should mention that had I been hired by the other airlines, I would have been in training when my father died and been unable to finish the courses. And even more important, I wouldn't have been available to my family in ways that I now see were necessary for this situation. We must always remember that our ego has a myopic view of life's unfoldment, so it's often a good thing when our ***ego prayers*** aren't answered affirmatively by Heaven.)

I flew down to Dallas and went through the interview process, which begins with a group meeting and finishes with a one-on-one session with a recruiter. After my group interview, I was sitting nervously in a room waiting, when a man with dark features finally came in, looking at my file. He glanced up and seemed a bit perplexed, then he said, "I see you're from Minneapolis. So am I . . . when I was a kid, my family and I used to go to this Greek church by Lake Calhoun. Have you seen it before? It has a gold top." I was in shock—this was the church from my dream, the one I'd seen on my run! I felt shivers go up and down my spine and thought this was a sign that the job was mine.

We had a great one-on-one interview, talking for about 30 minutes. Finally, he had to leave the room to get a piece of paper for me to sign, which stated that

I was willing to be tested on my French proficiency. I thought I'd be hired then and there. Heck, this was the significance of the dream connection, right?

The recruiter returned, and I signed the paper. Then I left the office, stayed with my aunt for the night, and flew back for my father's funeral the next day. Two weeks later, I got a rejection letter in the mail yet again! I couldn't understand why the Universe kept torturing me. My ego was all out of ***prayers,*** and I realized just how attached I'd once more become to getting this job. Yet again, I ***chose*** to ***accept*** that it wasn't what God wanted, and so ***surrendered*** to the greater plan—whatever that was.

Destiny . . .

The Minneapolis winter was approaching (I found the season depressing and brutally cold!), and I knew I wouldn't get through it with all that had just happened with my family, so I decided to move to Fort Worth and live with my Aunt Sandy. Once there, she got me a job waiting tables in her restaurant. Although the money was okay, it wasn't great because regular customers knew the other servers and would request them instead of me. I ***prayed*** for a little financial help from the Universe and used the ***Law of Attraction*** to magnetize a better source of greater income.

One night I went out on the town in Dallas and ended up at a bar where one of the bartenders happened to be someone I knew from Minneapolis. He told me that I should consider bartending there if I wanted to make some extra money. I realized that this was the answer to my ***prayer*** (what I'd attracted), so I knew I should consider it. But there was one catch: At this establishment, each night had a certain theme, and one was "underwear night"—so you know what that meant! That's right: I could only wear underwear that night while serving up those oh-so-refreshing beverages.

In the interest of life experience, I went for it, lasting a mere four weeks before I'd had enough of my ass being pinched and my crotch being grabbed while serving drinks! At this stage, I wasn't sure if talking to God would do any good because my last plea had gotten me into this mess, but I ***prayed*** anyway, asking the Divine to lead me out of the situation.

A few nights later, a customer from Chicago named Paul came in with a girlfriend of his, and having sensed my dissatisfaction said, "You're too classy for this place. You're not happy here, are you?" I was in a bit of shock—he'd just given me an intuitive reading. We talked about "underwear night" and how I couldn't stand it anymore, as well as the fact that most of my co-workers were on drugs. He then suggested I check out another bar a few blocks away that was popular and more upscale. As it turned out, the answer to my ***prayer*** had come from a stranger who eventually turned into a lifelong friend.

On my first day off the following week, I made an ***authentic choice*** out of my deepest integrity to go down the street to this other bar (where full clothing was mandatory and there was a "no drugs" policy) and check it out. I got hired on the spot as a doorman and floor worker (meaning I had to pick up everyone's empty glasses and trash). I had to work my way up to bartending there, but at least I got to keep my clothes on!

Although this was a better environment for me, a month went by and I found myself feeling lost, frustrated, full of despair, and unable to bear being part of the bar life in any shape or form. One night I was walking around picking up glasses and cigarettes when I started to break down inside. From the depths of my soul, I felt every part of my being powerfully rise up in me. Then internally I said to God, *Is this all You have in mind for me? Is this my "vibrational match"? Is this all I can give back to life? With all the gifts I have inside, how can this be it? What else is there for me, God? How else can I be of service? Is this all I was born for?*

I'd said a soul ***prayer*** and in that moment shifted my vibration to my highest potential, animating the ***Law of Attraction.*** I felt as though my entire being were flowing out through the tears falling down my face onto the floor and through that prayer. Five minutes later—and I mean that literally—I was checking IDs at the door when a man with dark features walked in. He looked incredibly familiar, yet I couldn't figure out why.

I let it go, and then the end of the night arrived. As was our ritual, I walked up to the bar and did a shot of liquor with all of my co-workers. I looked to my left, and standing at the bar was the man I'd noticed earlier. Finally I asked, "Do I know you from somewhere? You look very familiar to me."

He exclaimed, "You look familiar to me, too!" We spent about five minutes trying to figure out why we recognized each other, and after it seemed we'd exhausted all the possibilities, it hit me: He'd conducted my one-on-one interview for American Airlines.

"You're a flight-attendant recruiter!" I exclaimed.

"Yes, I am!" he replied.

I told him that we recognized each other because he'd interviewed me, to which he asked, "Did we hire you?" I told him no, and he couldn't believe it. A friend of his then came up, and they left the bar. I drove back to Fort Worth that night wondering, *What is God up to?*

The next night, the recruiter came back into the bar, found me, and said, "Listen, I'm sorry I left so abruptly last night because of my friend, but something doesn't sit right with me about us not hiring you—do you mind giving me your social security number so I can find out why?" I was in shock. I said yes, of course, and gave him the information.

He told me that he'd call me within a week and let me know what he found out. He kept his promise—five days later I heard from him. He'd discovered that there had been a mistake during the screening process. After my one-on-one interview, my file had gotten mixed up with someone else's—I should have been hired! He then offered me a chance to re-interview, and I was given the job on the spot! It turns out the significance of my gold-topped church dream finally revealed itself after all.

I'll never forget that period in my life. It was one of the most profound times I've ever experienced because it was the first instance as an adult that I'd come to know my soul and understand the Divine beyond New Age dogmas and fantasy. During that entire experience, which encompassed nearly two years, I was humbled in ways I'd never known before. I learned about true humility, ***surrendering*** to cosmic timing, making ***authentic choices*** based on integrity, the true power of ***prayer,*** and where the ***Law of Attraction*** is effective. If the sequence of events had happened in the way my ego had wanted it to and I'd been hired earlier by American Airlines, I later figured out that I would have been based in Boston instead of Chicago. In that location, I wouldn't have crossed paths with some very important people.

I also found out that our prayers are always answered by the Universe—but often not in ways we'd like them to be. The Divine won't take away our lessons but will help us learn them. Sometimes we must go through a severely challenging time so that we can clarify who we really are. How else are we going to know our true character without having it tested? I discovered that sometimes the only way to work with Fate is to accept it and ride it out.

As you continue reading this book, you'll discover and explore the many agreements you've made with Fate. Some of these can't be changed because they serve as necessary limits that comprise your life's unique blueprint. These boundaries keep you on the path your soul chose for this lifetime and can't be changed once you're here. Sometimes your Fate can shift, but it's all a matter of timing. And sometimes you unconsciously create your own obstacles and Fate yourself.

Nonetheless, your agreement with Destiny does indeed ask you to discover the formative spaces where you're free to choose how you'd like to create. These lie within the limits of your Fate and are the areas where you get to manifest your life as a co-creator with the Universe. The tools you've learned about so far—***acceptance, authentic choice, surrender, prayer,*** and the ***Law of Attraction***—deal greatly with moving past the ego to the soul to transform the Fate of your life into Destiny.

With these tools, you're now ready to confront Fate, no matter how it shows up in your life, and transform it into Destiny. Not every situation you encounter requires all the tools. Nonetheless, sometimes they all become necessary to carve the Destiny out of the stone of your Fate, like a sculptor bringing forth the *imago* (visualized image) out of a marble slab.

Therefore, as you keep reading, make sure all your techniques are handy. In each section that follows, you'll be educated on aspects of your Fate, given an example of how it can show up in your life, and then asked to apply what you've learned to effect change and fulfill your agreement with Destiny.

Let's begin first by investigating one of the basic ways in which we all experience our contract with Fate: *through our mortality.*

PART II

Transforming Mortal Fate into Destiny

"Death is certain, and when a man's fate has come, not even the gods can save him, no matter how they love him."
— Homer

With our tools in hand, we're now ready to explore our first Fate—*Mortal Fate*—and how our soul has agreed to transform it into Destiny. It's only fitting to begin here because this is what we first encounter during our incarnation and birth. Take a moment to envision what it was like for your soul to make an agreement to be bound to a mortal life.

Imagine that before you're born your soul meets with the guardians of the earth, which I'll call *the Fates* from now on. As they prepared you to incarnate, they inform you that entering this world demands that you participate in the evolutionary process, laws, and this dimension's structures of time and space.

Your soul says, "Cool! I've always wanted to study creation at Earth University. Let's do it!" (Although you may often want to attend a different "college" once you're here!)

The first step in determining how you'll embark upon this heroic journey is choosing the body you'll be born into. In essence, that becomes your first experience of this world. This vessel is comprised of genetics, ethnicity, race, gender, appearance, size, shape, instincts, and even the ancestral memories contained within your cells.

As you go before the Fates, they hold a council with your soul, members from your soul group, and your team (as mentioned before, this includes your spirit guides and teachers). The purpose is to decide what would best serve your growth, as there are innumerable options regarding the body that could be assigned to you. After discussing what specific way in which you'll work with Creation this time, and which body best serves this purpose, they devise the perfect lifetime for you to consider. Yet they caution you: *Know this, dear soul: Every path requires that certain limitations be put in place, and these will manifest as aspects of your Fate on Earth. They are designed to keep you on track with your soul's intention and purpose—your Destiny. And some of these limits will be found in the very body you inhabit.*

Once you've made your choices, the Fates assign the necessary karma to keep you from creating through the same patterns as the last time you incarnated. Then the Fates inform you that the natural laws of this particular world must also be honored in order to fulfill your creative quest. This includes abiding by the cycles and rhythms of Earth and its nature and the final fate of the body: death.

Even though the end of life on the physical plane is a reality we all must face, it's not the end of our consciousness, just the body we've used to fulfill our creative journey. This is not unlike the soul deciding to put down the paintbrush it was creating with, which has come to the end of its usefulness in this world.

When the process is complete, it's time for your physical incarnation. This demands that you forget your other lifetimes and what Heaven was like. Those who have had near-death experiences often describe the "Other Side" as a place filled with cosmic love. Do you think you want to remember *that* while searching for just a little stable mortal lovin' this time around?

Our true identity and how it has incarnated and reincarnated must remain one of the greatest mysteries of life so that we can create anew. We're left, then, with only our Mortal Fate to initially guide us once we're here which it can, if properly understood and respected. Unfortunately, forgetting that our true origins are found in the eternity of the spiritual world often renders us quite frightened once we're here on Earth. We're most certainly scared of our own corporeal death, and therefore of a concept like Fate.

So before learning how to transform our Mortal Fate into Destiny, we must first face our fear regarding Fate. What causes us to be such a Fate-phobic culture and deny the very nature of life and death as two sides of creation? Furthermore, why are we unable to accept the limits that come with our bodies: the fact that we age, get sick, and lose others through death?

Answering these questions is essential to our Destiny. We certainly can't begin to transform Mortal Fate until we understand the source of our fears around the entire concept. In fact, *it's our pervasive cultural fear of Fate that keeps us from using the limits of our mortal lives as sources of direction and clarity of purpose.*

Chapter 7

MORTAL LIMITS AND OUR FEAR OF FATE

"Know thyself, nothing too much."
— Greek saying

At Apollo's temple in Delphi, Greece, the above precept—the first part of which is transliterated from Greek as *"Gnothi Seauton"*—was inscribed over the portico in gold letters. To *know thyself* and *nothing too much* doesn't mean spending countless hours in meditation and therapeutic self-analysis. It simply means knowing your limits, embracing who you are, and not striving to be something other than that. It also means: Don't overstep the terms of your mortal contract with the Universe; know that your ego isn't immortal and you must accept the soul's agreement with the Fates to work within particular boundaries.

When you were born, you were fated to certain mortal limits. If you don't honor them, you won't be able to perceive the borders of your life, and thus will be unable to find your center. This will render you a lost soul on this planet without a Global Positioning System for your life.

Coming to *know yourself* must include working diligently toward an awareness of the limits established by your Cosmic Contract. While some of those (which we'll investigate later) are less obvious and more difficult to ascertain, with your Mortal Fate what you see is often what you get. Unfortunately, most of us don't want to look! Rather, we'd like to think that we somehow aren't really bound to mortality in irrevocable ways. This becomes the basis of our Fate phobia—we simply don't enjoy the idea that aspects of our lives may have already been set in celestial stone.

Speaking of which, some years ago I was having dinner with a friend after teaching a yoga class, and we were discussing our favorite subject (the meaning of life!). I asked her, "Do you believe in Fate?"

She gulped and almost dropped her fork. Looking more panicked than I'd ever seen her, she blurted, "No! I just can't believe there are things in life that are predetermined. I believe in destiny."

"But doesn't the word *destiny* imply predetermination?" I pressed. "And if not, how do you define destiny?" She explained that, to her, the term implied that she could determine the course of her future from unlimited possibility.

Her startled, fearful reaction left me truly puzzled. Couldn't she recognize that within her own life, limits were needed to give her a certain trajectory? Since then, I've come to realize just how pervasive this fear of Fate really is in our Western culture.

But what's making us so afraid? The question intrigued me, and I began to write articles and do research on the subject, which led me back into studying our collective past. I discovered that although death has rarely been a desirable reality, no matter what the time period, not all cultures of antiquity feared it as much as we do today. And everything related to our fear of Fate in all of its forms is sourced from our anxiety regarding change and death.

Confronting Our Cultural Fate Phobia

In my investigation of our collective fear of Fate, I was led once again to the ancient Greeks for a deeper understanding. Unlike us, this culture not only generally embraced Fate, but they thought that it dignified the human soul. Greek consciousness, mythology, and philosophy were saturated with the idea of Fate.

Hesiod, one of the first religious poets in Greece, thought that the laws found in nature were just and exact. He felt that it was humanity's duty to understand, learn from, and honor these precepts because we're each a part of the natural world. He also believed that death, *the final Fate,* should be respected as a law that issues from a Divine source.

In addition, like the Three Fates that held high status within Greek mythology, the Greeks revered the goddess Moira (pronounced *Moy-ra*). The Greek word *moira* means "allotment," and this deity was charged with the task of assigning certain limits as a necessity for the soul's journey on Earth. It's from Moira that we find the origin of the word *hubris,* which implies arrogance, exaggerated pride, or self-confidence that defies the gods and our fated limitations.

Moira symbolized the sum of the Three Fates and was considered a "minion of justice," always ready to punish those who, through hubris, would overstep their contract with the gods by transgressing natural law. To avoid this, the Greeks felt it wise to understand, study, and embrace nature's limits. Furthermore, this idea of natural law draws on connections to the fundamental feminine principle of life we still call "Mother Nature." This system therefore represents all that's found in nature: the processes of birth, death, seasons, cycles, aging, and time.

From the environmental destruction that we're causing on a daily basis, it's clear just how divorced we are from the concept of natural law. Even our obituaries avoid labeling the cause of a death as "natural," opting instead for descriptions such as "heart failure," "liver cancer," or "stroke." And let's not forget all the ways we run from the reality of aging!

As I studied the Greeks and their worldview regarding Fate, something began to stand out. I started to make the connection that their portrayal of Fate was primarily through female images, which were Divine in their own right. In fact, they worshiped goddesses as well as gods. As I then looked at our historical process and our currently popular definitions of God, it became clear that the deities we collectively worship today resonate with the patriarchal power structure of our times. Most people relate to the Higher Power as a *male* force. Simply put, we live in a culture that lacks a belief in God as a feminine force that holds equal status with a masculine one. Let's face it, we don't pray to *our Mother who art in Heaven!*

If we conceive of God solely as a masculine deity, how has that shaped *our* worldview regarding Fate? In portraying the Fates as female deities, were the Greeks on to something that now speaks to our pervasive Fate phobia? Is this the by-product of living in a world where God is only a *He?* Is honoring the Divine solely as a male force sabotaging our Destiny?

Let's look deeper into this to understand why the Greeks connected Fate to the feminine aspect of the Divine and how we might do well to embrace the *feminine* force of creation as well as the masculine.

Fate and the Feminine

In her book *The Astrology of Fate,* Liz Greene sums up the connection between Fate and the feminine succinctly: "Perhaps one of the reasons why there is an inevitable association between fate and the feminine is the inexorable experience of our mortal bodies. The womb that bears us, and the mother upon whom we first open our eyes, is in the beginning the entire world, and the sole arbiter of life and death."

In other words, it's through the feminine, which is our mother, that we first experience limitation via our corporeal existence: our physical bodies. Once born, our souls become boxed into a structure that has its own DNA coding and laws—this is an aspect of our *Mortal Fate.* Not only do most of us fear the death of our bodies, we also dread and fight their limitations. As our physical selves are connected with the feminine principle of life, we therefore fear that, too, and in doing so we disconnect ourselves from one half of creation and God: the Divine Feminine.

I can't begin to speak to how much this affects us all—men and women alike—polarizing us against our own wholeness. We not only struggle against the limits of our bodies as meaningful, we resist our sensuality, our sexuality, and the social empowerment of women. It's no accident that females all around the world—the embodiment of the Divine Feminine—are marginalized, bought, sold, beaten, raped, and even murdered for stepping outside the patriarchal dictates that hold them as second-class citizens in their own countries.

Given the Judeo-Christian roots of our Western culture, it makes sense that women hold a lesser place in many sectors of our society—and that we are a society that struggles with loving the earth, our bodies as they are, our limits, our sensuality, and our sexuality. My eyes were most opened to this by a college course in Native American philosophy where I learned that for many Native American peoples, Earth *Her*self was part of the miracle of creation and life. She was their Great Mother, and they sought to live in harmony with Her, understanding that they were Her very eyes, ears, voices, and children.

In this same class, my Lakota professor mentioned that when the Puritan settlers arrived, with their beliefs that Earth was a place of penance because Adam had been led astray by his female companion (Eve), the Lakota looked at the settlers trying to divide and own the land and asked, "How can you own the land? The land owns you!"

Learning this allowed me to see the clash of ideologies that still plays out in our own relationship to the earth, our bodies, Fate, and the feminine face of God. Furthermore, we can't underestimate the hold our Judeo-Christian perspective *still* has on us and how we relate to these things. For example, our fear of the feminine and Fate even shows up in New Age concepts and spiritual literature. Drawing on the teachings of the Buddha, some misguided teachers claim that the world we live in is false and illusory and will vanish once we awaken to our immortal selves—a concept quite like the Christian notion of the Last Judgment.

I couldn't disagree more. When the Buddha said that this mundane world was an illusion, he was trying to teach the deception of permanence, that nothing is forever on this plane, so let go of attachment! Furthermore, he taught that we shouldn't identify our whole selves exclusively with this existence (the ego). Although we're part of this world, we are not *from* it. Earth is a temporary *expression* of eternity, just as our bodies are a fleeting outer expression of our eternal souls.

We must learn to love our physical selves and this planet and honor them, in spite of having been told otherwise by various patriarchal religious doctrines. After all, we dwell in the bodies—and on the soil—that Mother Earth has loaned to us as part of the soul's journey, do we not? If we continue to dishonor Her, She may turn on Her children through forces of nature to save Herself. Based on the climate crisis we're witnessing, we can see that we're already on borrowed time.

To begin to heal, we must first face our fear of Fate that issues from a dread of limits and death, which, in turn, have been projected onto feminine aspects of life. Respecting Mother Earth, embracing women as equal to men in all areas of life, and giving God a feminine face are crucial to unfolding our purpose—each of these actions connects symbolically to our soul's agreement to transform Mortal Fate into Destiny.

Furthermore, the Destiny of our Mortal Fate is, in part, to affirm that we agreed to incarnate into the physical self that we have for a meaningful purpose. As long as we refuse to acknowledge this, we sabotage our own empowerment and direction. In fact, this denial has become the source of much self-hate for many people. That said, let's evaluate more specifically why we chose the body we did this lifetime as part of our Mortal Fate.

Chapter 8

SELECTING AND ACCEPTING YOUR BODY

If you read the accounts of those who've had near-death experiences (NDE), you'll find many common themes regarding the selection of our bodies and our Mortal Fate. Most of these individuals report having been shown by guides or angels that almost all of their experiences on Earth, including their own bodies, were chosen out of necessity for their soul's growth.

Betty J. Eadie gave a full, detailed account of her own NDE in her book *Embraced by the Light,* in which she dedicated an entire chapter to "Selecting a Body." She writes that as each of us made the selection of a body and a family with which to incarnate, "we understood the . . . physical and behavioral attributes we would receive from our families. We were aware of the genetic coding of mortal bodies and the particular physical features we would have. We wanted and needed these . . . and we were confident in accepting these circumstances."

To be in harmony with this part of our Fate while here on Earth, it might be helpful to realize that we don't create our bodies or our family per se; we leave that up to the Universe and the Fates. Rather, it's my sense that our soul is presented with some options to choose from and then agrees to be *assigned* what best serves its mortal purpose. Yet we're so out of harmony with this particular component of our Cosmic Contract that once we're here, we get stuck in our ego and often spend most of our lives rejecting the assignment!

I'll use myself to illustrate this: I'm a white male, 6'1", and 195 pounds. These physical parameters were chosen by my soul to best serve its original intention in this lifetime. This body has given me limits of operation. For example, I can't decide that I'd like to be an Olympic gymnast. The Fate of my current incarnation simply won't allow this to be my Destiny—especially at my age (although I did give it my best shot until I grew past 5'10" when I was 16).

The Mortal Fate of my body was woven into my life's purpose from my very first breath. Even though I'm a great athlete, I was never *meant* to be an Olympic gymnast—a Fate I must accept as guidance toward my Destiny. I could have spent countless years denying this, and most likely would have endured many injuries serving as fated course corrections.

Take a moment and extrapolate from my example something that applies to you. In which ways do you reject the body that your soul chose? Do you do so because of a cultural spell that tells you what to find beautiful? There was a story in *Time* magazine a few years ago that provides a perfect example: In rejection of their appearance, many adult women and teenagers in South Korea are having blepharoplasty (eyelid surgery) so that their eyes look more round. Instead of accepting their heritage, many believe that looking more "Western" is the key to advancing in their own society and being beautiful.

Because of this cultural spell, they've created a perceived disadvantage for anyone who *doesn't* have the surgery! And what will be expected of future children, whose DNA dictates that they'll be born with the same Asian eyes that the grown-ups surgically changed? Will each subsequent generation have to keep getting operations in order to be empowered and accepted? As a result of resisting their Mortal Fate, these individuals have created a madness that could amount to billions of dollars wasted on something they fundamentally can't change. Could they apply those wasted resources to other things that would empower their souls instead of this cultural spell?

I'd like to share a story from my client files that demonstrates how someone I worked with transformed the Fate of her body into the creative Destiny of her soul once she finally began to accept it. Meet Jessica.

Jessica: Mortal Fate Embodied

Jessica had many issues with being a woman and came to me for a reading after years of struggling with bulimia. She'd sought out all traditional forms of therapy and treatment, yet none of them had helped resolve her compulsion to eat and then purge her food.

When I tuned in to Jessica and began to intuitively read her Cosmic Contract, I received impressions that her soul had chosen to be born female in this lifetime for a very important and creative reason. I sensed that she'd incarnated on Earth before as a man who hated members of the opposite sex and subjugated many of them to various abuses, using his societal authority as a priest. I could sense rape, beatings, and selling women as part of her soul's experiences in that past lifetime. The priest's loathing seemed to stem from his having been abused and shamed by his mother.

To be clear, when I receive past-life impressions from clients, I don't interpret them too literally. How the hell do I know if they really were these people? But what I *do* take seriously is their symbolic importance. That said, I realized that in *this* lifetime, Jessica had a subconscious resistance to her female body, and she was manifesting this through the very act of refusing to *nourish* it! Thus, the true source of her bulimia was a soul issue, not a mental or emotional one. No wonder traditional therapies didn't work for her—it's not as if a clinical psychotherapist was going to talk about her Cosmic Contract and past lives.

Her soul wanted to learn how to create differently in this lifetime and bring overall balance to her experiences on this planet. Although she'd accepted the gender assignment on the Other Side, she was fighting it once she got here because it was a new pathway for her soul. That struggle was manifesting as bulimia: a compulsion that denied the nourishment of her female body. And as I progressed through the reading, I also began to intuit that she had numerous problems relating to other women and that most of her relationships and friendships were with men.

When I sat down with Jessica and began to relay my perspective on the true source of her bulimia, she was astonished. She confirmed that she hated being female and that she naturally got along better with men. In fact, she was unable to forge friendships with other women that didn't end in some major power struggle.

Curiously, Jessica told me that she felt drawn to comparative religious studies, which she'd explored as an undergraduate. However, when we met for the reading, she was working on her Ph.D. in women's studies! The one thing holding her back from receiving her doctorate was her dissertation: She couldn't figure out what to write it on. When she told me this, I got an intuitive hit to direct her toward researching religious influences on the cultural subjugation of women. I also received an impression that she should begin a yoga practice.

A year later, I got an e-mail from Jessica. She'd become a new person by using some of the tools for transforming Fate into Destiny. After our session, she told me that she sought out a past-life-regression therapist and worked toward ***accepting*** her contract with Mortal Fate to be embodied as a woman this lifetime. In addition, she made a ***choice*** to start a yoga practice, which helped her connect to her physical self. She healed her bulimia within three months, and as I'm writing this book seven years later, she hasn't relapsed.

Jessica also wrote that as she ***surrendered*** to her soul's choice to be female in this lifetime, she began to connect to other women and had already made two genuine friends in her yoga class. She told me that my guidance about her academic troubles had been the answer to a prayer she'd said before our reading, and she'd just finished her dissertation on the influence of Christianity and women's cultural roles in Western society!

How do *you* waste energy, time, and money trying to change your Mortal Fate instead of embracing it? What is that costing you in terms of your resources and your soul? Where are you denying the guidance toward your purpose that your body is giving you? How is that manifesting? Do you think that you're too tall, too short, too wide, or too thin? Do you wish that you had blue eyes instead of brown or white skin instead of black? Can you ***accept*** your body as it is, as something your soul ***chose*** for specific and creative reasons? Can you honor those reasons through your inner authority?

Once we're in our bodies, there's more to Mortal Fate than just our gender or physical shape. During our entire lives we must negotiate the ways in which we change with time. Yep, now we're moving into the cultural spell of youth that has us all by the short hairs. So how do we transform the Mortal Fate of time and aging into Destiny? Well, it begins by putting things into perspective and realizing that aging is a gift and a privilege, not a curse, as I'll discuss in the next chapter.

Chapter 9

TRANSFORMING THE FATE OF TIME AND LOSS INTO THE DESTINY OF WISDOM

I remember picking up a local newspaper some years ago, and a front-page story had the headline "Plastic Surgery: A Cure for the Midlife Blues." With all that was going on in the world at the time, I was irritated that this article merited not only the prime spot, but also a five-page interior spread that chronicled the writer's decision to have extensive plastic surgery (which was given freely as trade for the doctor's exposure in the paper). This was ostensibly done to assuage the depression the journalist was experiencing at the age of 50 because she was no longer getting noticed in singles bars, and she was always being told that she looked *tired.* It was like reading an episode of *Sex and the City!*

I felt compelled to write a letter to the editor (which was published), stressing the reality that we're all under a *cultural spell* that has warped our ideas about what's really important. I urged the author of the article to go visit a burn-victims ward in the nearest hospital to get some perspective—oh, yes I did!

Now that I'm ten years older than I was when I wrote that letter, I have more compassion for the woman, but my stance hasn't significantly shifted. As I watched my body change with time, I, too, began to wonder how I might eventually seek to turn back the clock and avoid this aspect of my Mortal Fate. But the sudden death of one of my best friends, who was only 33 years old, shook me out of my own cultural spell and clarified my own perspective about aging.

As I sat at her funeral, I realized that I'd never get to see her grow old. In that moment, I embraced what a *privilege* aging truly is, especially when others die so young that they never get to see the wrinkles of life taking shape on their faces . . . those like my friend Jenny.

At the end of the day, what does aging mean to individuals who have cancer and are hoping to live long enough for their daughter's next birthday or their son's high school graduation? Many people in this world would give anything just to see one more line form on their skin. The wrinkles on our faces show where our souls have been on Earth. The tragedies of life are there to remind us that aging is a privilege, not a curse.

Although the media bombards us with messages that cause us to reject what we have in favor of being younger, thinner, and prettier through surgery, cosmetics, and dieting, there are few messages that show us how to work with and honor the bodies we've been assigned. It's here where we must apply the tool of ***acceptance*** if we're to use our Mortal Fate as a vessel of Destiny. To be sure, even the most ancient cultures established codes of beauty. But if we look more deeply, we discover that generally, these standards weren't primarily based on rejecting the body. Instead, they were a way for the people to align themselves symbolically with the deities they worshipped.

When it comes to the Mortal Fate of aging, we must first *embrace* it as a blessing, not a curse, in order to transform it into Destiny. We must begin to shake off the pervasive cultural spells that brainwash us into running from aging, change, and death—and ultimately fleeing from life. If we keep trying to forge eternal youth on Earth, we'll never be able to authentically graduate into a society that once again reveres its elders as *wisdom keepers*.

Unfortunately, we live in a culture that has lost all regard for the concept of age as something sacred. No longer are we able to look into the faces of our elders, see their wisdom wrinkles, and be guided through their wise counsel of life experience. Rather, we tend to avoid them, shoving them into nursing homes so that we don't have to see what lies ahead for all of us. We forget that older people are still growing *toward* something and awakening their souls into this world.

Without elders who act as wisdom keepers for our culture, we can't know where our collective soul has been and where it's headed. We'll continue to elect leaders who don't know how to take us forward to higher ground. When we're focused on keeping everything the same, we can't appreciate the wrinkles of wisdom that the collective soul wears on its face. This world is fated to constantly change—just like our bodies—no matter how much we try to paralyze it with Botox. To act otherwise is to live a lie.

Sadly, we've all seen those who have had extensive plastic surgery as they try to run from aging, and the reality is that they often don't look younger or better.

They just look like people who have had a lot of plastic surgery—without any real authenticity, without a soul.

The cult of youth, which has spun the current cultural spells of beauty, has programmed us against loving our own bodies in an authentic way. We've lost the sense of what it means to be *authentically embodied,* and without that mortal integrity, we can't anchor the soul into our lives. Although this seems to be most obvious with women in our culture, we must also be aware that it affects both women and men alike. In fact, men are now being diagnosed with what's being called the "Adonis Complex"—an addicted focus on body image that often results in countless hours spent at the gym and getting various plastic surgeries, such as pectoral implants or liposuction, to meet a six-pack-abs standard of beauty. I'd like to share a story about a client of mine who fell prey to this cultural spell; meet Tom.

Tom: Facing the Truth

Seven years ago, back when I saw clients in person, Tom scheduled a reading because of relationship problems, among other reasons not related to body image. When I intuitively evaluated him before he came to see me, I sensed that he was a very strong man—full of character, charisma, and the qualities of a leader. But I also picked up that he derived too much of his confidence from his good looks.

I tracked in his psyche that this was the result of his mother only focusing on that quality as he grew up. Since he was only superficially valued, this was the only way he knew how to feel self-worth. This showed up as a major dependency to which he lost a lot of power.

When Tom arrived for his session, I saw that he was, without a doubt, a good-looking man. In fact, he could have been Superman's twin brother! As the reading progressed, I shared that I felt he might rely on his looks too much, and I asked him what he was going to do as he aged further. (He was already in his early 40s.)

Tom confessed that he'd already had liposuction, teeth veneers, two chemical face peels, and rhinoplasty (a nose job). At the time, I felt that all of this enhanced his beauty, and it wasn't noticeable to the naked eye—he actually looked great! But with my inner vision, I saw that this man wasn't done and would find himself in a major crisis before long.

We concluded the session, and five years went by before I heard from him again. Once again, Tom came to see me because of relationship troubles, yet I knew that he was returning because he needed some counsel regarding the latent issues I'd briefly touched on the last time. And although by this time in my career I'd stopped seeing clients in person, Tom asked if we could meet again, and I agreed.

When he showed up, I barely recognized him. Gone was the confident, handsome Superman look-alike. Instead, an insecure man who'd had a lot of noticeable plastic surgery stood before me, and he still consciously felt that he just needed counsel with respect to the end of a relationship. During the session, I finally looked at him and asked, "Tom, you do know that you're not really here to talk about this woman you're thinking of leaving, don't you? Do you think there might be another reason you were adamant about meeting me in person?"

He looked at me with a blank stare, and then asked, "Robert, what do you mean?"

He'd opened the proverbial door for me to get to the real issue, so I walked right in and said, "Your soul has brought you back to me because it's time you faced the fact that you're scared of losing your good looks to aging. You're terrified because you've derived so much of your esteem and confidence from your appearance that it has become the foundation of what you value about yourself."

This was hard for Tom to take. He protested for a few moments that he looked great and that others still thought of him as a Superman look-alike. He was unable to acknowledge that since our last reading, five years earlier, he hadn't taken the time to develop a new value set—one appropriate for a person approaching 50. He hadn't done any work on finding other qualities to value besides his good looks, and he was bereft of soul-esteem.

Finally, he confessed that as things began to sag, he woke up one day and decided he needed to get his eyes done, which led to his first face-lift the following year. Then two years later he had another, more severe, face-lift.

I asked Tom if he thought that his surgeries were noticeable and he said no. But they were very apparent—he didn't really look like himself anymore. All I could see was a wounded man, externalizing his lack of inner worth through multiple plastic surgeries, trying to outrun his fears of losing all of his worth to aging.

Our session came to an end, and I could sense that Tom was going to leave his failing relationship, which was a good thing for him to do. But when I asked if he was planning on having any more "work" done, he paused and then said, "I'm sure that in five years I'll need to get everything touched up."

As he left, I knew he'd be getting more surgeries in the near future, and that he wasn't going to turn the Fate of his self-esteem into the Destiny of soul-esteem . . . something that everyone but him could also see right there on his face.

Are You Under the Cultural Spell of Youth?

We can't change the fact that we age. It's my sense that as long as our culture focuses on trying to alter the things we really can't—without a predominant focus on the things we *can* transform—we're doomed to lives that are Fated instead of Destined. We become more concerned about the latest wrinkle treatment than how we can truly make a difference for others.

I want to give the subject of aging particular focus because we resist this Fate so much that it has hijacked our cultural soul. Long gone is a reverence for the face of an old grandmother or grandfather. We don't take the time to listen to the stories of their lives; instead, we're more concerned with what the latest trust-fund "celebutante" or pop princess is doing.

I must be honest in saying that I like my wrinkle creams and have to challenge my own misperceptions of what it means to get older. I'm under this spell, too! But I hope to inspire you to explore the ways you run from this Fate that pushes your soul out of your life. I don't think the soul minds our eye creams, but I sense that multiple elective plastic surgeries might not be what the true self prefers. Imagine what the money spent on these procedures could do for those without enough resources for *lifesaving* surgeries and basic health care.

Take some time and use the following exercise to evaluate this aspect of your Fate, and if you are transforming it to Destiny. Ask yourself these questions to discover how much you're under the cultural spell of youth, and write your responses in your journal. If you answer yes to any of them, you may want to refocus your thinking. Transforming Fate into Destiny requires an acceptance and appreciation of your body as it is *now*.

- Do you see your face as a renovation project?
- Do your aspirations for your face and body dominate your thoughts?
- Do you wish that you looked like someone else?
- Do you fret over how others perceive you?
- Do you define success in terms of youth and appearance?
- Do you deprive yourself of enjoying certain activities because of how you look right now?
- Do you resent your body for "letting you down" by showing signs of aging?
- Do you spend more than you can afford on skin-care products that promise to reverse the signs of aging?

- Are you considering cosmetic surgery to try to roll back the clock?

When it comes to our mortality, there are certainly other Fates that we must also learn to perceive as blessings—and some are certainly more difficult than accepting the aging process. How can we learn to see the death of a child, a terminal illness, a disabling accident, or a natural disaster as a blessing? How do we transform that Mortal Fate into Destiny? Can we do so? Well, yes, we can.

Let's look at how one client I worked with did just that, turning her loss into a gain. Cindy contacted me for an intuitive reading as I was in the process of writing this book. I was feeling a bit stuck about how, out of the hundreds of clients I've worked with, I was going to select the story that would best embody how we're each called upon to take the sudden tragedy Mortal Fate often brings and extract Destiny out of it.

When it came time for me to call Cindy for her appointment, I had this strange sense that there was going to be something very significant about her reading, but I couldn't put my finger on what it was. I kept getting the feeling that maybe she'd want to write about me. And although I thought I'd already intuited most of the significant points about her, I would soon discover that there was one crucial thing that hadn't registered on my intuitive radar screen.

I already knew that she'd come into this life to be a host and build community and to network for others. I understood that a powerful guiding force was assisting her because she was working on something that would help many people—in fact, I was overwhelmed by this presence. I then intuited that she was struggling with some sort of creative project and taking over its vision by stepping in as more of a directing authority, which was challenging her lack of self-confidence (a vestige from her childhood).

She also had a contract with Fate to experience some pretty harsh events that seemed related to her family. What I realized (well into the reading) is that *I* was actually the one who was going to be writing about *her* and the profound way she transformed her Mortal Fate into Destiny.

Some People Die So That We Might Know How to Live

When Cindy told me that on April 10, 2003, her son, Danny, was killed in a car accident a half mile from her house, I was stunned. This is the sort of thing that I normally pick up on before I call someone for an intuitive reading—and the fact that I didn't know about it was a signal to me that I needed to pay special attention to her story. As it turned out, I was being given something important that I needed for this book.

The day he died, Danny had left their house with one of his friends, who was an inexperienced driver. As they drove down the street in a caravan with other friends, the driver of the car Danny was in lost control while going 67 miles per hour. The vehicle slammed into a tree on the passenger side, where my client's son was seated. Danny died at the hospital shortly thereafter.

Cindy went on to tell me that she always *knew* her son would die young. She believed that his soul had made that agreement with her. And she knew that his death was not in vain—*Danny had died so that other people would know how to live.* Cindy said, "There were many lives that changed as a result of Danny's death. We call these changes *Danny's Gift.*"

After he left this life, the outpouring of support from her community was so overwhelming that she knew she had to do something to honor her son's spirit. So she and her husband took this Fate and transformed it into Destiny by founding a youth center and calling it "Danny's Place" (**www.dannys-place.org**), which finally opened on March 13, 2006. This organization focuses on helping teens develop character assets that will prevent them from participating in risky behavior. Talk about Destiny!

I was very touched by Cindy's journey. As she told me about Danny's Gift to her, she said, "I found my voice and my spirituality and have gone from being a stay-at-home mom to the president of a nonprofit corporation. My husband started volunteering. My daughter wasn't shy anymore; and she learned about compassion, hope, anger, sadness, joy, and other essential values in life."

Cindy's story defines how we each can use the tragedies that Mortal Fate often brings as catalysts of Destiny—whether they show up as fatal accidents; terminal illnesses; or the loss of loved ones through suicide, murder, or natural disasters. Cindy told me that she had many, many things to ***accept, choose, surrender to,*** and ***pray*** for during the past few years—not to mention the fact that she had to forgive the young friend who was driving Danny's car.

Transforming Mortal Fate into Destiny may be one of the hardest tasks that we encounter in this life. But if we don't find the silver lining within our human limits, we won't learn how to work with our Mortal Fate and open up new possibilities for our future. We must first be able to perceive each negative event that comes our way as integral to the rest of our journey and the destination the soul is pointing toward.

Eventually, we'll all face our final Fate, making the agreement we've formed with Destiny all the more urgent. For we simply don't live forever, and although we may come back to create again on planet Earth—should She accept us—we only get one shot at creating through this current life. Destiny asks us to make the most of it!

Although the next part of our journey together will enrich and edify us about where we've already been, the focus must shift. Destiny is the way in which you're called to use your Fate in ways that have never happened before and will never occur again. Only *you* can live this unique Destiny you've agreed to. But our Fate isn't just defined by our mortal limits—it also includes other psychic dynamics through which we often can unconsciously *fate* ourselves.

PART III

Transforming Self Fate into Destiny

As you embark on this next section, you'll be making a considerable shift, and I'll provide you with a new map to guide you. You'll still need the tools you've learned about in the previous chapters, but you'll be applying them to different aspects of yourself.

You now know that Mortal Fate has to do with the necessary limitations, experiences, and events that your soul chose and that you often can't change, but must ***accept*** and use as guidance. Self Fate, on the other hand, is a much different agreement that the soul has made and offers more ***creative choice.*** It has its particular boundaries, however, so I'll help you build on your knowledge.

Transforming Self Fate into Destiny is more about confronting how we create our own challenges in life by not understanding and accepting our inner psychic processes and patterning with respect to our physical and mortal limitations. As we'll see, this is where we can create our own Fate in this life via self-imposed limitations. These cause the Universe to send Divine interventions our way in order to wake us up.

Such situations often manifest in the form of difficult people, synchronicities masquerading as "accidents," creative obstacles, and fated redirections. You're about to find out that you indeed *can* change the course of your future through an awareness of what's inside of you and what you decide to do with that inner impulse and treasure.

But before you get cookin' here, you must have an in-depth understanding of how psychic processes work in this regard. As I map your psychic terrain, I'll provide examples to ground the concepts. I'll then explore how to implement techniques for evaluating your Self Fate and the ways it mirrors what you don't recognize in yourself and how it serves as an initiation into your soul through what I call *the dark night of the ego.*

However, first we must move beyond understanding the mortal ego to something far more complex that the ego is fused to: *the psyche.*

Chapter 10

ANATOMY OF THE PSYCHE: EGO, SOUL, AND SHADOW

Once our consciousness has been born into a body on Earth, it's contained not only within that physical structure as part of a mortal life experience, but also in something that reaches beyond this plane into the world of patterns, energy, and intention—it's called *the psyche.*

From *psyche,* we derive the word *psychology,* which actually means "soul wisdom" or the study of the soul. This implies that by understanding and examining our psyche we first begin to know the soul. It has agreed to be contained within the structure of consciousness—the psyche—which functions as a temporary container for both the ego and soul while we're alive.

Furthermore, the psyche is inextricably woven into the earthly process of time and cycles, as well as all that's timeless and eternal. Yet it matures and develops in ways that often mirror our body's process of growth. As we age, the psyche can open up new conduits in the ego structure that allow the soul to have an increased influence on our sense of identity.

Diagram 1 shows the various layers and structure of the psyche in the way that I've intuitively come to perceive it. When I do a reading, I sense all the levels that lie beneath ego awareness and how they inform and influence my client's self-concept.

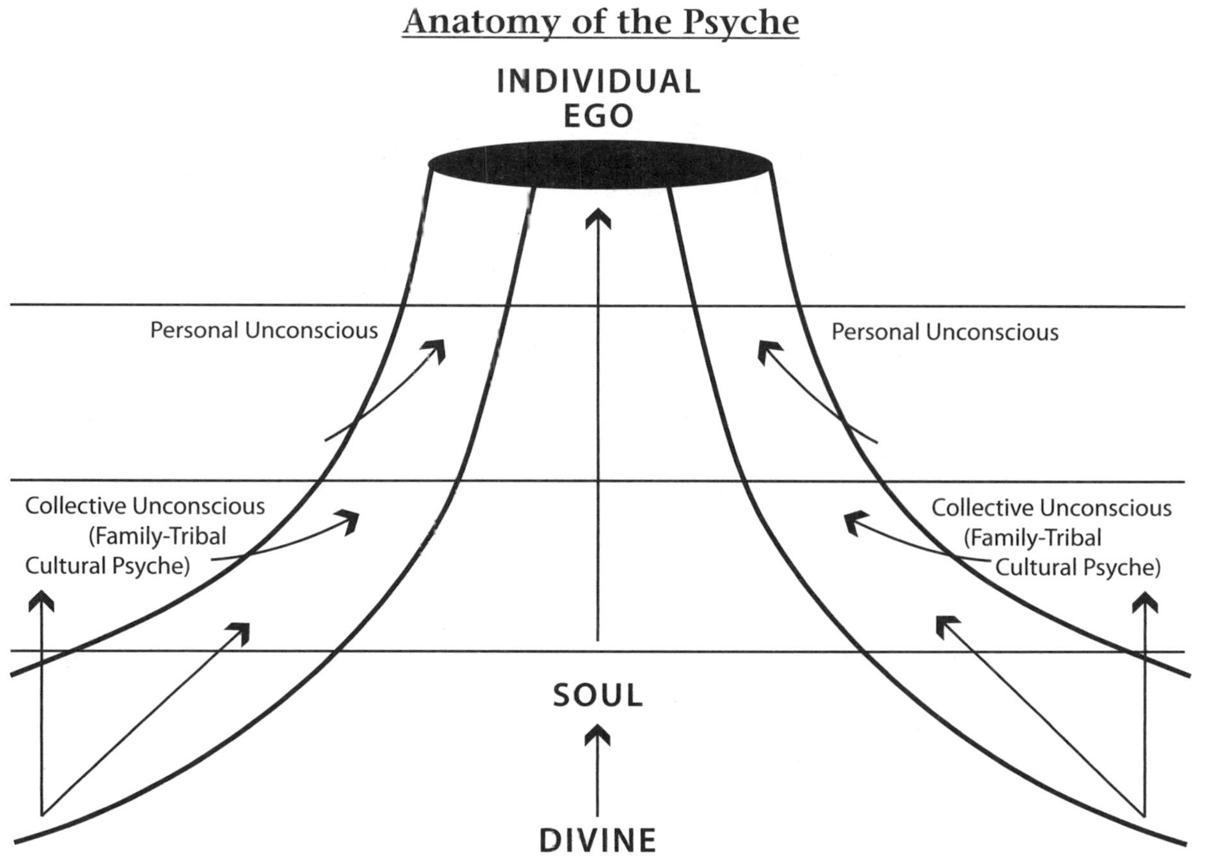
Anatomy of the Psyche
INDIVIDUAL
EGO
Personal Unconscious
Personal Unconscious
Collective Unconscious
(Family-Tribal
Cultural Psyche)
Collective Unconscious
(Family-Tribal
Cultural Psyche)
SOUL
DIVINE

As you can see, the ego sits at the top of many other layers, which all function in tandem with it. In order to define Self Fate and transform it into Destiny, we're going to dive down into the depths beneath the ego, sinking beyond it toward the soul. As we do so, the first section that we encounter is called *the personal unconscious.*

The Personal Unconscious

As we're born into this life, our soul's consciousness is too powerful for the tiny infant body and brain that it's fusing with, and thus only a small part can incarnate and begin to interface with the process of ego development and the outer environment. The ego starts developing at about age two as we break from fusion and identification with our mother, and it then commences to manage our reality. This breaking away from our mom is the first step we take in our emancipation as individuals and often manifests as "the terrible twos."

Yet the ego isn't actually the main force in directing consciousness within the psyche, although it often likes to think so! There's something much more powerful guiding our ego development from within, and this is where the rest of our soul's consciousness resides: *the personal unconscious,* which lies beneath ego awareness. It's not only the unknown part of the psyche, but also the gateway to our soul, true origins, dreams, and subconscious mind. The latter is contained within the personal unconscious and is accessed and programmed during certain forms of hypnosis because it believes and acts out whatever we program into it, acting like a computer by storing all experiences and interfacing with the body itself.

To begin a process of self-realization in earnest, we must learn to dialogue with the personal unconscious and all of its contents. But it doesn't speak the language of the rational mind; it uses the language of the soul, which is primarily a symbolic form of communication via our dreams and imagination.

Conversing with the personal unconscious is the first step we take in speaking with our soul. To get there, we pass through a lot of uncharted terrain. We enter into a realm of ourselves that's unknown to our ego, and although it's frightening, we must make the journey. It's here that we access our connection with the Universe and the secret of our purpose, making it crucial in transforming Self Fate into Destiny. For the personal unconscious contains something of great power that must be negotiated as we come to know our soul, and that can be a source of much Self Fate if it isn't understood: *the shadow.*

Self Fate and the Shadow

The shadow—greatly explored by the brilliant Swiss psychiatrist Carl Jung—is the part of the personal unconscious that's a repository for uncivilized, repressed, suppressed, or unacknowledged aspects of ourselves. These include impulses, aspects of the soul, and other components of our nature that haven't been expressed, embodied, or integrated since early childhood and adolescence—often because our ego, family, religious institutions, and culture didn't approve of them.

The development of the shadow happens in tandem with that of the ego. As the ego structure develops (your self-concept), our parents, peers, culture, religion, or government don't consider certain things acceptable for outer expression and personality integration. These disowned parts of ourselves are pushed down into the personal unconscious, thus creating the shadow. Examples include obvious negative traits such as selfishness, deceit, lust, jealousy, greed, or aggression—things that we don't want to admit because doing so would threaten our idea of who we are.

Subduing these qualities isn't necessarily a bad thing, because if we didn't contain some of our darker impulses, a civilized society and life wouldn't be possible. Imagine what would happen if we each acted out our anger after an airline cancelled our flight! However, repression is only effective at containing the lesser drives of our humanity when it's a conscious process that doesn't turn into *denial,* in which we disown these aspects as if they aren't part of us.

This is very important to understand when it comes to transforming Self Fate into Destiny. In fact, I've often found that what I'm primarily doing in readings is seeing into clients' shadows, the parts of themselves that they won't acknowledge. Further, I'm perceiving how this part of their unconscious is now showing up as a form of Self Fate because it simply wants their attention!

For example, I've done many readings on women who greatly repress their need to express anger in a healthy way—a natural emotion, to be sure. Yet because they deny that they have this very normal feeling, it shows up as the Self Fate of passive-aggressive behavior or depression. Their ego—often because of sociocultural conditioning—can't absorb the reality that they're human and are going to feel mad! And because of this, the rage has no other option but to come out in a shadow form as Self Fate.

But this isn't the only way we self-fate through the shadow. It must also be understood that even though our ego is initially greatly shaped by the outer world as part of our acculturation, it also needs to be informed by what exists in our interior—the innate disposition that we've carried into life via our soul (although this can remain an unconscious factor).

None of us arrives on Earth *tabula rasa*—as a blank slate—onto which our family and culture exclusively draw our identity. We come here with all sorts of gifts, talents, and inclinations, and you can often see a glimmer of this natural-born wealth gleaming in the eyes of young children. *But even these very positive qualities and talents can be forced into hiding by parental, religious, or social conditioning*. When this happens, these components become part of the buried treasure hidden within the shadow—bounty that we must mine when the time is right so that it may take its rightful place in our lives as a wealth of creative allies.

These two factors—the denial and repression of negative traits that our ego refuses to integrate and keeping qualities of the soul hostage in the shadow—set up the main ways that we fate ourselves. Thus, understanding these two processes in depth is vital to the transformation of Self Fate into Destiny. We must thoroughly unravel the mysteries of the shadow, so let's first look deeper at how the dark part of ourselves is created by denying the impulses of our soul.

How the Shadow Is Created

In Diagram 2, I've mapped out how the psyche functions when it's forced to repress something issued from—and innate to—the soul, something that's meant to incarnate into the ego. As this component of the soul rises up for recognition and integration, it's evaluated based on the ego's allegiance to outer authority. In looking at the diagram, you can see how the shadow is created by the ego repressing parts the self back into the personal unconscious when it's in allegiance to outer approval. Once again, inner authority becomes crucial to the liberation of the soul into this world.

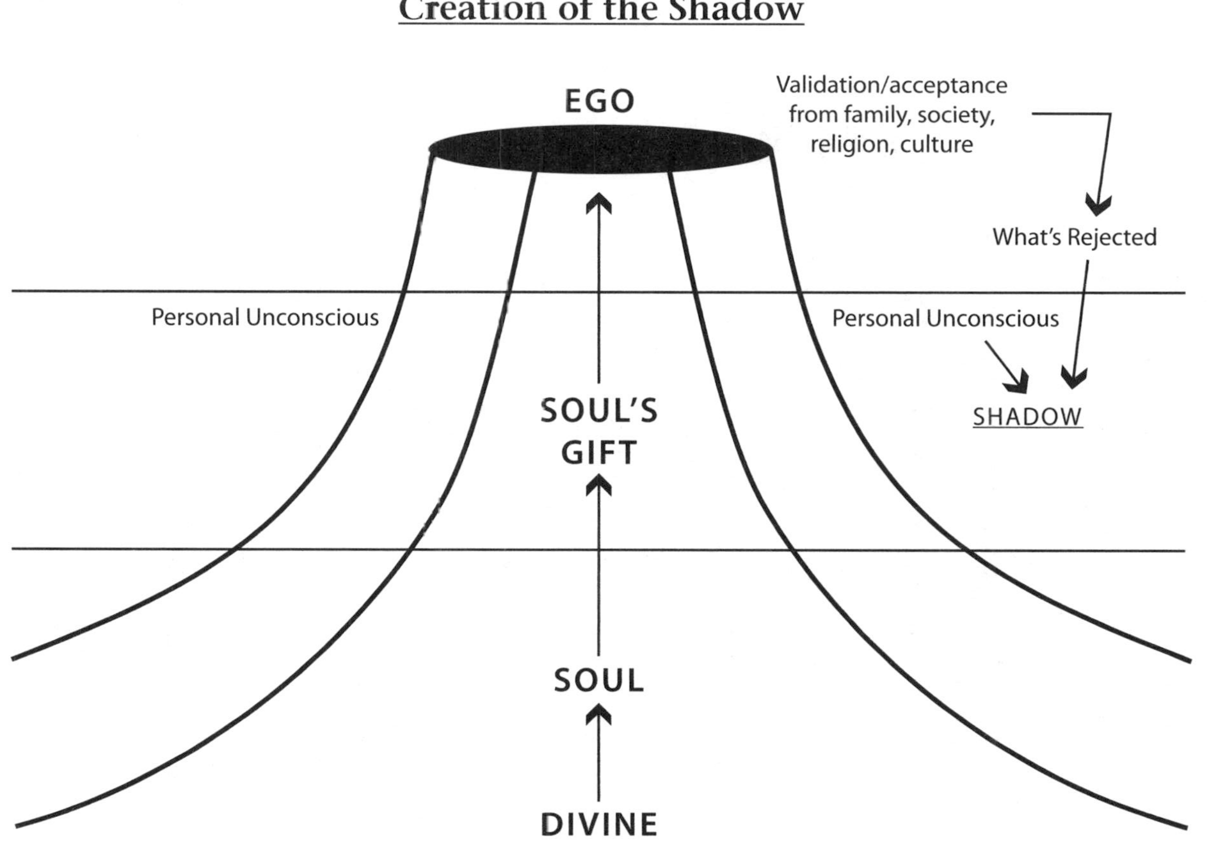
Creation of the Shadow
EGO
Validation/acceptance from family, society, religion, culture
What's Rejected
Personal Unconscious
Personal Unconscious
SHADOW
SOUL'S GIFT
SOUL
DIVINE

When these disowned pieces are denied, there are a few ways in which they try to get our awareness—because they aren't going to go away! As the saying goes: "What you resist, persists." Well, not only does it keep coming back, if it's continually repressed, it gets stronger and manifests in increasingly extreme and sabotaging ways. At the end of the day, the ego is no more successful at shutting down the contents of the personal unconscious—including the soul—than we are at stopping a hurricane.

Although all sources of your identity are filtered and coordinated by the ego, it's really a servant to the deeper soul's identity. Therefore, the ego can make a big mess of things when it believes that it's the center of consciousness within the psyche and can keep the shadow and personal unconscious under control. Let's look at an example to see how this happens.

John: Living a Shadow Life

Six years ago I did a reading for John. His story demonstrates how he'd come to terms with his Self Fate and transformed it into Destiny via a dialogue with his shadow. He came to me as he was turning 40 because, as he told me, he'd been maintaining two lives and wanted to make them one. John had one existence for others, and the other path—the one he now wanted to bring into light—was his *shadow life.* The psychic toll this split had taken on him had Self Fated him into a deep depression.

When I read his psyche, I detected that in spite of being married to a wonderful woman and having two kids, John was primarily sexually attracted to men. I intuited that he'd been brought up in a strict religious home where being gay was not only considered immoral, but his parents actually told him that they'd kill him for it!

In addition, the boys in John's family weren't allowed to exhibit any "girlish" traits, yet he innately possessed them. I sensed that he'd brought a very developed feminine side into this life when he was born—it was simply part of his nature and soul and a true gift to his integrity as a man. It also became clear to me that my client had been a very emotionally sensitive child growing up.

I felt that John's soul had chosen this family in order to experience what it truly meant to create a life of authenticity. His soul had agreed to break a legacy of generational repression through a Fate of incarnating traits and desires that were so deeply denied by the family psyche.

John confirmed that he'd been attracted to men since he was six years old, and that he had, indeed, been a very emotional child. He recalled that his father had verbally abused him, calling him "sissy boy" and making fun of the way he spoke, which made him self-conscious. Because of this, he became very quiet and reserved and developed a stutter, while his ego began to repress his feminine side.

Years later, when he felt called to pursue a career as an interior designer, he became an architect instead, suppressing his innate urge in favor of a more "masculine" profession. And at 26, John married a woman he'd met in college, even though he knew it went against his inner nature. Throughout their marriage, his repressed self began to manifest as a shadow life, which included frequenting various *dark* places for anonymous sex with men: parks, bathrooms, and adult-video stores. He sought me out for a reading because he felt that he was hitting bottom and realized that his life was in crisis. In addition to having a naturally feminine side, he was also innately gay.

What I sensed in John left a lasting impression on me. He had an incredibly creative soul that he was unable to authentically incarnate because of certain cultural, religious, and institutionalized family values. As a result, he found himself at the mercy of the very part of his nature and Fate that he'd denied for so long and that could only be lived out in an extreme shadow form of disconnected, soulless encounters with other men in dark places.

As I charted his cycles of growth, I knew that the time had come for John to begin integrating his unclaimed self before he seriously harmed himself by remaining in this split state. He was clearly in the grips of some serious Self Fate. He was already in a *psychic* crisis, and I knew that it would manifest as a physical issue if he didn't heed the guidance of his soul.

Shortly after the session, John came out to his wife and released what was hidden in his personal shadow for conscious integration. And even though he felt better, there were still other challenges ahead. A year later, we had another session, and I gained profound insight regarding the nature of the shadow and *the collective psyche* as they relate to Self Fate and Destiny.

Shadows and the Collective Unconscious

When John came back for his second session, a little more than a year after our first meeting, he told me that after having repressed his sexual self for so long, he'd gone out to openly explore the gay community. But he reported that he still felt incredibly lost and disconnected. Through his initial experiences, he'd been disappointed to discover that, generally, this new culture was overtly focused on sex, which was spiritually disempowering. John found no men who fostered the deeper emotional connections within physical intimacy, which he craved. Society has long defined gay men solely via whom they sleep with—in other words, only as sexual beings. In turn, many gay men internalize this and make their sexuality the focus of their lives.

As I pondered my client's statements, I intuitively charted him in this new psychic field and began to sense that the gay community itself was built out of the shadow of the larger social psyche. This taught me that the shadow not only operates at the level of the individual, it functions within the collective psyche, as well. Furthermore, when we begin to investigate what lies in our personal shadow, we also step into the darkness of our family, cultural, national, and global psyches as well. In fact, the contents of the personal shadow are often a by-product of these other, larger psychic containers and their processes. Thus, quite often what manifests as our Self Fate can be the result of larger dynamics than just our "stuff"! Using John's case, let's look at this more deeply via the American psyche, or America's ego.

In his reports during the 1940s and '50s, Alfred Kinsey established that the American psyche can't integrate the fact that many people are more sexually ambiguous than they care to admit. This is born out of a Judeo-Christian belief that sex outside of marriage and same-sex connections are sinful. Influenced by such thoughts, many men and women who have homosexual feelings (which don't necessarily mean that they're gay) project those feelings onto gay men and lesbians and then vehemently speak out against them. This strengthens the speakers' self-concept of being exclusively heterosexual so that they feel "free of sin" and acceptable to God and society.

However, when someone "doth protest too much," we know that a shadow dynamic is at play. Each individual's darker self then amalgamates into a collective shadow. And in order to become authentically empowered, every gay man (such as John), lesbian, or transgender person must negotiate breaking free from that group influence.

Although my client had managed to free himself from his family's psyche, he became stuck in the legacy of a sociocultural shadow. Ironically, this dark power was perpetuated by the choices and behavior of many gay men through their lack of authentic sexual rapport with each other. It wasn't until some years later, when he was in a serious and loving relationship with another man, that John embraced a new Destiny of feeling whole, liberated, and authentically grounded in his sexuality.

He had two Fates to negotiate: (1) being gay in a homophobic society that shamed him into denial of this part of himself; and (2) joining a group that replicates the projections of the dominant culture and thus fates itself.

It's my sense that the reason American society is so afraid to allow gay marriage is that doing so would symbolize the movement of gay men and lesbians out of the cultural shadow into a more integrated and conscious part of the country's ego and psyche. This would set a precedent for *all* minorities seeking greater inclusion in the psychic power structure of the United States and would rattle the current elitist system to its bones as it changed laws and policy nationwide!

Even those who aren't homosexual can gain much from John's story because we all internalize cultural psychic processes and thus create our own Self Fate. His experience shows how we integrate the unconscious structures around us and fate ourselves to a disempowered life when we're unaware of the dynamics of oppression. This should give pause to other minority groups who seek to distance themselves from the gay-rights movement, claiming that it's not a civil-rights issue. It is. Women, African Americans, Mexican Americans, Asian Americans, Native Americans, and all other minorities in the U.S. are disempowered and often perpetuate that situation through the same pattern.

Take a moment and think about how you fate yourself by replicating the same power issues and struggles of culture. How has society labeled you, and do you believe it to be true? Do you act out those stereotypes and fate your own life? Taking this further, John's story points to something else that informs our personal unconscious and shadow: *the collective unconscious.*

The Collective Unconscious and the Fate Point

"The psychological rule says that when an inner situation is not made conscious, it happens outside as fate. That is to say, when the individual remains undivided and does not become conscious of his inner opposite, the world must perforce act out the conflict and be torn into opposing halves."

— C. G. Jung

When most of us begin working with the personal unconscious, we never imagine that we've just stepped off a cliff into the swirling depths of the collective. Awareness of this can make the process of knowing our shadow loom larger—it seems to be a dark and daunting task. For when we invite this part of ourself to dinner, we've often brought a collective darkness to the table as well.

As we go into the personal unconscious and move deeper, we enter into a larger psychic field known as the collective unconscious. This is the psychic matrix that exists beneath the awareness of the various social and cultural egos we're fused with. It's important to understand how we're connected to this layer of consciousness because here is where *the collective shadow* can be found, which contains the rejected impulses, traits, and buried treasure of the different social and religious groups, states, or countries existing on the planet. Yet it's unlikely that anyone would willingly sit down and spend time with a table of collective demons!

Given that perspective, it's easy to see why it usually takes an intervention by Fate—perhaps a deep dissatisfaction, depression, accident, or difficult event—to make us venture into the shadows. Intuitively we each know that the "rabbit hole" inside of us can extend into forces and issues larger than, yet still connected to, our own. Thus, we must also consider that this action of Fate is often not only the by-product of rejecting our own shadow, but also the shadows of the groups we participate in. (We'll soon explore this and how it fates us, too.)

Still, taking responsibility for knowing and owning our own shadow is paramount and our first step. In fact, it's crucial in transforming our Self Fate into Destiny. Put simply, not doing so sets us up to fate ourselves because *whatever we don't own in our shadow has no other option than to eventually externalize as Fate, until we acknowledge and integrate it back into ourselves.*

In other words, when we repress, resist, ignore, and deny the negative parts of ourselves found in our shadow for long enough, there will eventually come a moment of truth that I call the *Fate Point.* Diagram 3 illustrates this process.

The Fate Point

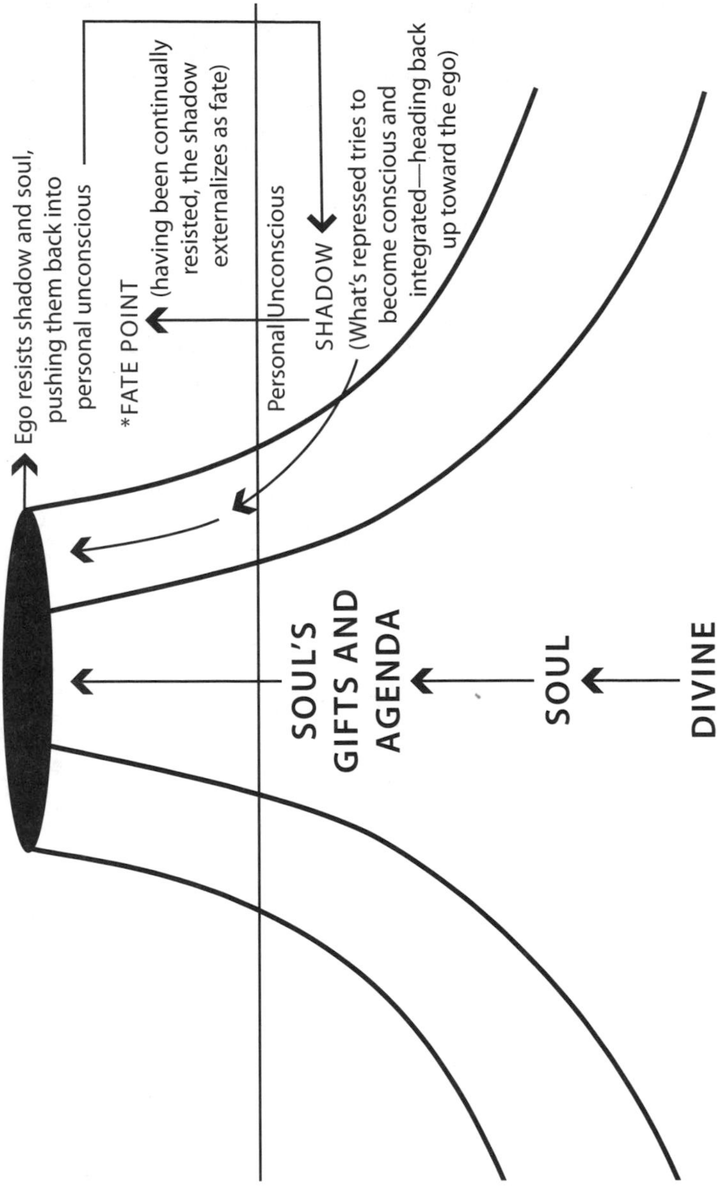

EGO

Ego resists shadow and soul, pushing them back into personal unconscious

*FATE POINT

(having been continually resisted, the shadow externalizes as fate)

Personal Unconscious

SHADOW

(What's repressed tries to become conscious and integrated—heading back up toward the ego)

SOUL'S GIFTS AND AGENDA

SOUL

DIVINE

The Fate Point is our Self Fate's point of origin and occurs when whatever we've been resisting in our shadow finally becomes a fated part of our lives to be experienced in a variety of ways. And boy, can this process be creative in its manifestation! But no matter how unconventional it seems, the Fate Point relies on a universal law called *synchronicity* to fulfill its end. Now you may think of this concept as meaning mere coincidence, but it's much, much more . . . and it's an ingredient of Self Fate that must be understood for you to transform it to Destiny.

Synchronicity's Role in Transforming Self Fate into Destiny

The term *synchronicity* was coined by Carl Jung, who defined it as "an acausal connecting principle that differs from mere coincidence as it implies not just a happenstance, but an underlying pattern or dynamic that is being expressed through meaningful relationships or events." That can seem a bit wordy. Jung was trying to say that he felt that the events in our lives occur in tandem with the processes of our psyche—the inner connection of the ego and personal unconscious. Thus, synchronicity stems from our psyche's interrelationship with the Universe and the laws of creation, not as a causal factor, but as a mirror.

For example, Jung was known to recount the following story of his friend Richard Wilhelm in explaining his view of synchronicity. Wilhelm claimed that this story was true and that he'd witnessed these events firsthand. He was stationed in a small provincial Chinese village that was experiencing a long drought—pushing the village toward the edge of starvation. After having exhausted all the prayers and rituals they could think of to bring rain, the elders of the village decided to recruit a famous rainmaker from another province to come to their aid.

Days later, the short and ordinary-looking rainmaker showed up in a horse-drawn cart. He immediately requested a remote private hut where he could be completely undisturbed, and he asked for enough food and water to last four days. For three days, no rain came. But on the morning of the fourth day, the villagers were awakened by a heavy downpour!

Wilhelm was in shock and quickly ran to the old rainmaker, who was preparing to go back to his province. "How did you make that happen?" asked Wilhelm. Grinning, the old man explained that he'd done absolutely nothing, but that in his own province, everything was in balance with the Tao (the Divine consciousness that connects us all). There, he said, it rains when it needs to, and when it needs to be sunny, it's sunny—all because those living in the region are in harmony with themselves.

This, he remarked, wasn't the case in the drought-plagued village. Here, the people were out of balance with themselves, and that put them out of sync with the Tao. When he'd first arrived, he recalled, he'd been thrown off-kilter himself because of the chaotic consciousness of the villagers.

He'd isolated himself from their lower state of being until he could reestablish the connection and harmony between him and the Life Force. And on the fourth day, his resonance with the Tao had been restored, which produced the rain as a by-product!

The moral of this story shows the deeper meaning of synchronicity, which is a natural universal phenomenon that manifests as a commentary on where we're in or out of harmony with ourselves. It's actually a wonderful aid in transforming Self Fate into Destiny. It mirrors what's going on inside us that we aren't conscious of or are forcing into our shadow and what will externalize as Fate to get our attention.

In other words, synchronicity points us toward Destiny, but often by midwifing Fate into our lives at precisely the right moment as a statement of where we're out of harmony with ourselves. Yet it can also show us when we're in perfect alignment with our soul. It reveals how our inner and outer lives connect and directs us to the soul's intention—but only if we're willing to see our lives *symbolically.*

One of the best examples I can offer regarding this phenomenon of synchronicity with respect to transforming Fate and Destiny is the way in which this book came to be! Originally, I had a contract to write on a completely different subject, but the Universe and my soul had a different plan in mind.

In August 2005, I signed on to write a book about my work with astrology. At the same time, I'd put together a lecture tour with Caroline Myss and my talk was entitled "Fate, Free Will, and Your Heroic Journey." I'd come up with this material because I felt it would be the best way for me to give something useful to attendees and offer some much-needed insight from my work over the years.

Several months later, things happened in my personal life that I'd come to realize were in *synchronicity* with my lecture—namely, the death of one of my best friends, Jenny, who was killed in a minor car accident, and my mother surviving a much more serious wreck (the stories I shared in the Introduction). This double shot of synchronicity was showing me something that I needed to see and absorb.

I spent the next month meditating on these events until the time came for me to give my first lecture on "Fate, Free Will, and Your Heroic Journey." My mother and stepfather came to Las Vegas for the occasion, bringing with them the photos of my mom's SUV after the accident. Quite frankly, she and her passenger should have died—there was very little left of her vehicle.

It was after that lecture, having received an overwhelmingly positive response from attendees and having seen those photos, that I intuitively recognized the symbolism and connectedness of the two events. I then knew the Universe was telling me to write *this* book instead of the one about astrology. And in synchronicity, the publisher mirrored my inner realization and agreed!

Of course, my choosing the lecture material had in no way *caused* the death of my dear friend or my mother's near-fatal accident. But the intuitive part of me knew that my choice to write a different book was woven into the threads of these events as part of a Divine plan—as part of my Destiny.

It's in our Cosmic Contracts that we agreed to be fused within certain patterns that we'll use to create our lives, as well as a Divine schedule. In addition to the beginning (birth) and ending (death) points on this schematic, another cosmically timed event is the moment at which some aspect of the self—for example, a creative project such as this book—is ready to be born. Synchronicity will point the way if we're able to see events as symbolically imbued with inner meaning. This is yet another reason why it's an integral part of transforming Self Fate into Destiny.

In addition, our relationships are an important area where we can use synchronicity in transforming Self Fate into Destiny. In fact, the people we're close to provide the most accessible synchronicities for beginning to understand what we need to see in ourselves and in our shadow. They can show us how integrated and healthy we are. There's no doubt that our connections with others can be the best mirror to gaze into for a glimpse of our darker selves. They allow us to awaken to our unconscious self in gentler ways that don't call for the Universe to hurl bricks at our heads—unless, of course, our relationships *are* the bricks!

That said, to use this resource, we must understand how we've fated ourselves to the relationships in the first place. I'd like to introduce you to a dynamic called *projection* and how it works with the Law of Attraction.

Projection

Projection is the phenomenon of putting one of our own repressed and unconscious qualities onto another person, and it's where most of us must begin our shadow exploration. We project and then react—*strongly*—to the projected traits or qualities. We don't realize that we may not be responding to the other person at all, but to a repressed and rejected part of ourselves. In very real terms, this other person is being used to carry something that's really part of us, and is often made into a scapegoat!

In most cases, the individual actually does possess some portion of what we're projecting, some small hook upon which we can hang our shadow projections. But rarely do they embody the characteristic as much as we think. In fact, the magnitude of our reaction is a good gauge for the degree to which we're doing this. If we experience a strong emotional charge—whether it's disdain or even admiration—there's a good chance we're projecting.

With that in mind, note that we don't just project our *negative* disowned traits onto others. Sometimes, we throw off positive aspects of ourselves that we aren't comfortable acknowledging. For example, a woman who can't come to terms with her desire to be her own boss may project this onto all the strong females she meets, either disliking the authority they wield over her and perhaps resenting them or looking to them as her leaders through eyes of admiration.

Conversely, when we're in a state of *observation* rather than projection, we're usually more neutral and unbiased in our views. It's only from that state that we can see others for who they truly are. For example, imagine you're at the grocery store and witness a couple having an argument where it's clear that the man is verbally abusing the woman. Observation would believe, *This man is arguing with this woman in a way that disempowers her.*

Projection, on the other hand, would think, *Look at this jerk! Why is he speaking to her that way? And her—what a wilting wallflower. Get a grip, honey. What's wrong with you? I just have to tell this guy what an ass he is and tell her to get a backbone!*

Observation just sees what's happening without being hooked into the story line, while projection will rile you up one way or another!

Another interesting dynamic is that we'll often act out others' projections. Have you ever encountered someone who sends you such a negative, funky vibe that the next thing you know, you've started behaving in ways that you normally never would—and which reinforce their thoughts of you? You start saying or doing things that are extreme and out of character, things that leave you shaking your head and wondering, *Why did I act like that?* The answer is projection.

But we should note that the way in which we manage those situations tells us how well we know ourselves at the soul level. Once again, inner authority and soul-esteem, a function of a healthy ego, are the primary determinants of how we deal with this process.

This problem is especially evident in those who become famous. Instantly, they receive the projections of millions of people they've never met. They're splashed across the covers of celebrity magazines, written about by gossip columnists, and talked about on the evening news, filling the fantasies of complete strangers who imagine all kinds of things about their private lives.

For example, actors who lack a certain "soul centeredness" can easily lose themselves when this happens; and many find themselves in crises of depression, addiction, or fast living. Yet, time and again, we see that those who have a developed inner center are able to weather their fame with grace, staying grounded in their authenticity while avoiding the perils of self-inflation.

Working with Projection in Your Life

Whenever you find yourself receiving projected energy from others in ways that disempower you, step back and take refuge in your soul, knowing that a fissure in your ego structure is rendering you vulnerable. You're hooked into the projection because some part of you is unconsciously in allegiance to outer approval instead of to your soul. This gives your consent to become what others think you are, which can be a source of Self Fate!

For example, if I told you that I thought you were a zebra, you'd laugh at me: You *know* you're not a zebra, and my authority can't overrule your own because you're not vulnerable in this area of your ego. Yet what if I told you that I thought you were inarticulate (which could be a projection of my own insecurities)? Unless you'd established a certain amount of inner soul-confidence, you might actually find that you weren't able to speak that well when you were around me—fumbling sentences and using bad grammar. In addition, you'd be upset by my perception: Your self-esteem would take a hit, and you'd begin to lose even more personal power. How's that for a dose of Self Fate?

You can apply this idea to many of the things that people say about and to you to better determine just where your soul-esteem and inner authority may be lacking, leaving you vulnerable to transforming into what others think of you. Conversely, you must also take responsibility for the ways in which you disseminate and empower rumors you've heard and for harboring negative thoughts about other individuals or groups.

More positively, this psychological phenomenon also accounts for why we love to be around the people who see the best in us. They're projecting, too, but they're sending out the highest potential they see in us. And what do you know—we find ourselves acting that out, too!

Take a moment and think of when you've been around people who see and project only beauty onto you. Notice how you love spending time with them as they put you in touch with Destiny. This is because they affirm what's best in you, in the same way that it's uncomfortable to be around someone who, you can sense, thinks badly of you.

In this regard, projection is one of the most powerful acts of Destiny we can truly engage in—when it's used consciously—particularly when we put a positive thought onto someone else. Try it out: Go and project things onto people on purpose, and see if they don't act out some element of what you're doing. In fact, make it a daily practice to send someone that grace—especially a person you find it difficult to like—and watch how their behavior shifts for the better when they're around you. For example, you can do this with a difficult co-worker, child, or boss. Simply hold the image of their highest potential (it's easier when they're not around!) without saying a word about what you're doing. You'll be surprised—even amazed—by what can happen. For even if *they* don't change, *your experience* of them will.

Holding positive space for others in this way helps midwife their souls. It's powerful alchemy, to be sure, so we must all use it wisely. Don't say I didn't warn you! Now how does this all relate to the Law of Attraction?

Projection and the Law of Attraction

The Law of Attraction feeds projection because it simply causes *like to attract like.* On the surface, it may seem as if opposites attract, but projection shows us that we're more like that "opposite" than we care to admit. Inevitably, we'll draw to ourselves that which is most resonant with both our conscious self-concept *and* unconscious shadow.

You already know the types of people who affirm your ego—most often they're your friends, loved ones, and family. In order to be whole, you must also understand that your adversaries and those who annoy, irritate, and berate you are also telling you something about the energy you unconsciously emit. In this case, it's a force that's co-creating your life experiences. Perhaps it's fating you to certain relationships because of unclaimed territory within you, which certain people are mirroring back. Not only are we each attracting individuals into our lives in this manner, but we're often drawing in groups, too, since we're connected to the deeper psychic layer of the collective unconscious.

Understanding how projection and the Law of Attraction work when it comes to our shadow gives us the chance to see this part of our psyche and its buried treasure via the relationships we're in. I call this process—becoming aware of ourselves through the art of projection as it manifests in the relationships synchronicity has brought to us—*shadow dancing*. Are *you* ready to dance?

Chapter 11

SHADOW DANCING

Borrow the beloved's eyes.
Look through them and you'll see the beloved's face
everywhere. No tiredness, no jaded boredom.
"I shall be your eyes and your hands and your loving."
Let that happen, and things
you have hated will become helpers.
— Rumi

We've discovered that when we don't recognize or accept certain parts of our own nature—positive and negative—we'll project these qualities onto others. So now we must figure out how our relationships can take on new meaning so that we can use them to transform Self Fate into Destiny. It's through the dynamic of projection that we initiate a *shadow dance* with other people until we integrate what we're denying back into our self-concept.

Shadow dancing can often play out in our lives as a type of Self Fate. Surely most of us have had moments when we shrugged our shoulders in exasperation because we seem fated to draw such losers—oops, I meant difficult people!—into our lives. Even though we may be unconsciously fating ourselves to certain relationships, the good news is that this Self Fate can change into Destiny through conscious awareness.

Projection is an important component of shadow dancing because it sets up the dance itself. There's a Buddhist teaching that those who anger, irritate, frustrate, and even consciously attempt to sabotage us are our greatest teachers. Buddhists call them *noble friends,* because they mirror back to us the very things we most need to learn about ourselves. Always remember that in shadow dancing, *the other person is you!*

In other words, we're attracting into our lives individuals who hook us into a shadow dance in order to see *ourselves* more clearly. If, for example, you're incapable of owning your need to be assertive and self-directed, the chances are that you'll draw someone to you who bosses you around like a tyrant—or in extreme cases, who gets aggressive or abusive to motivate your inner warrior to surface. Or if you can't acknowledge that you're a narcissist and like to be the focus of attention, you'll attract friends who always want you to make them the center of your universe, without giving much regard to your needs.

Once we understand shadow dancing, it's difficult to continue doing it, because we can no longer claim the privilege of being a victim and blame someone else. When we catch ourselves caught in a such a dynamic, we're ready for—and required to accept—a new level of self-mastery and responsibility.

As a shadow dancer, you must assume that your dancing partner is teaching you something very important about yourself. This takes fearlessness, honesty, and accountability seldom found in our culture of blame, litigation, and hypocrisy. And I've watched many people focus far too much on the teacher in front of them, forgetting to concentrate on the lesson. They opt to resent and blame the one who's instructing them, instead of learning what they need to—sometimes for the span of their entire adult lives.

When we focus on blaming our noble friends, we miss the opportunities they bring for us to acknowledge the lesson and reabsorb the projection and help us transform our Self Fate into Destiny. As I said earlier, this doesn't mean that our dance partners don't possess *some* measure of the quality we're projecting onto them. But shadow dancing is really about self-discovery—leading us to the parts of ourselves that we don't know very well.

However, I want to be clear on something here that's very critical in how to deal with the negative aspects of yourself that you discover through this process. As you begin to recognize and identify unpleasant things, it doesn't mean that you should stop loving yourself. In addition, it doesn't mean that you should *act them out*. Venturing into your shadow and perhaps learning that you can be intolerant, judgmental, rude, and impatient or identifying that you're capable of violent thoughts doesn't mean that you should externalize what you find. (Did I just describe a day in city traffic, or what?)

Rather, the potentially harmful qualities that we find down in the shadow must be held in our awareness with compassion. And we'll uncover more than just the "bad stuff" through shadow dancing. We'll also discover what we need to express in order to feel whole as individuals, which we may project onto others to act out for us, fating ourselves to dependency. In this regard, let's look at an example of how we can unconsciously fate ourselves to experience certain relationships when we don't honor what's in our shadow. Meet Sally.

Self Fate in Relationships

Sally's story points to the conflict many of us experience as one of the most difficult challenges in relationships today: working toward wholeness when our society's marriage model teaches us to be someone else's "other half." Even the language of marriage demonstrates its role as a cultural spell. By that, I mean that we tend to say that we "get married"—period—rather than that we participate in a marriage. The latter implies movement, growth, and evolution. In addition, how many times have you asked someone who's married: "Where's your other half?" This demonstrates the fundamental illusion of the spell—that you need someone else to complete you. The marriage model also includes the illusory clause "Until death do us part." With nearly half of all legal unions ending in divorce these days, the reality is more like "Until we need to grow apart."

That said, Sally came to me for a reading because her marriage was in crisis. Simply put, she was tired of the shadow dancing that had been the source of her relationship's codependency. I could sense that Sally was playing the role of psychological caretaker to her husband, while he was emotionally distant and unable to reciprocate what she was giving. Consequently, she was frustrated and very resentful of him. She recounted years of feeling unseen, unloved, and unappreciated.

Sally communicated to me that she'd tried for years to get her husband to open up emotionally and engage in their marriage, which he'd resisted every step of the way. As the session progressed, I asked, "Have you ever considered that the two of you are acting out qualities for each other that you both possess—albeit unconsciously?" She looked blank. I continued, "In other words, you're carrying his emotional self, while he shoulders your need for independence and freedom from constant attachment."

I could sense that there was an entire other half of my client that she had yet to explore. This was because it had been forced into her shadow via the cultural expectations of what it means to be a married woman (or a woman in Western society, period). Sally had yet to creatively engage other aspects of her nature, ones that she projected onto her husband and he lived out for her. He, in turn, projected onto her what he'd forced down into his own shadow—the emotional and nurturing parts of himself.

This gave rise to the current crisis, catalyzed by the fact that Sally was ready to take responsibility for her shadow and projections, but her husband wasn't. Their marriage was at a choice point. I tried to help her see how she'd co-created this Fate with him because she hadn't been aware of the parts of her nature that had been socially repressed. At age 50, however, she'd gained the tools to bring them into the light. She was ready to integrate these unclaimed facets of herself.

In a follow-up session a year later, she told me that she'd separated from her husband six months after our initial reading. When she tried to communicate her new perspective and needs to him, he refused to listen and continued to disown his "other half," which he'd been projecting onto her. Yet, two years later we had a third reading in which she told me that they'd gotten back together!

I could sense that the separation proved quite useful and served as an initiation for her husband into his shadow. For when Sally left the marriage, she psychically handed back to him the disowned parts of himself that she'd been carrying, and he finally had to feel something on his own. There simply wasn't anyone available to carry the projection of his unclaimed emotional self any longer. Six months after their separation, he was hit by a deep depression, which prompted him to finally deal with his emotions and seek help. After three months of psychotherapy, he asked Sally to go to counseling together, to which she agreed.

During their time apart, Sally was hardly idle. It was good for her, too, because she was given the space and freedom to take care of herself and focus on activities that opened up her creative side. She took a trip to Italy with her daughter, learned archery, and went out with her co-workers every Monday night.

In the end, both Sally and her husband transformed their relationship Fate into Destiny, as they realized that in order to be whole, they each had to integrate their needs for emotional intimacy and independent freedom as valid parts of their being. I love this story because it has a happy ending. In fact, both of them attended one of my workshops, and I eventually gave them a couple's reading as well. (Unfortunately, most of the client stories I can tell that are similar to this one tend to end much differently.)

This is a wonderful example of the ways in which we *fate* ourselves to relationships where we must shadow dance to see the qualities that we're unconscious of in ourselves. Sally's story also illustrates that what we repress is often the result of cultural spells and expectations.

How Do You Relate?

Take a moment to look at and then journal about your relationship history: Can you see where you've fated yourself into certain dynamics? Have you ever shadow danced within both ends of this spectrum, such that in one situation you were the clingy caretaker, rescuer, and parent to someone else—while in the next you were more emotionally removed and feeling trapped by someone's perceived codependent neediness, which only seemed to stifle your need for adventure and freedom?

Seeing your intrinsic needs and identifying which one has been repressed and projected out is the first step. The next is to come up with a creative solution for how all those aspects can be integrated into your life.

And although this is just one example of the kind of work we must do to manifest a Destiny out of our Self Fate, we can draw much from it and apply it to the various ways we might shadow dance with others. Often, it's only when we can see what's being mirrored back to us through the dance—whether it's our negative traits or unclaimed needs to self-express—that we can awaken conscious choice regarding who we love and draw into our lives.

When we have that, we can manifest an *interdependent* relationship by magnetizing stronger, more spiritual relationships—a mirror of our own well-being and spiritual growth. After all, our relationships can only ever be as healthy as we are. Furthermore, our relationships and shadow dancing are integral to knowing our darker side, and they present us with a very important opportunity to befriend this part of ourselves.

Befriending the Shadow

"Within everyone there is light and shadow,
good and evil, love and hate. In order to be truthful,
you must embrace your total being. A person who exhibits
both positive and negative qualities, strengths and
weaknesses is not flawed, but complete."
— Deepak Chopra

Befriending the shadow is a terrifying notion, for we know that what we discover deep down in our darkness may conflict with our carefully constructed self-concept. As a consequence, the ego resists this kind of integrative analysis. It's so much easier to keep projecting our darkness onto others—and as I mentioned, venturing into this territory will require a new level of self-responsibility that most of us resist.

So why do it? Not only does knowing our own darkness allow us to see another's with compassion; it also opens us to all of the creative aspects of the soul that are hidden within this part of ourselves. Therefore, to befriend the shadow is to befriend the soul.

Paradoxically, when we manage our own darkness and own it, the purest light is able to shine through us. This means that not laying claim to our capacity for negative action and thinking that we're only *good* will inevitably own us, shoving our soul out of our life, while inviting Self Fate. This is especially important for those of us on a spiritual path, questing for the "light" and reaching for Destiny.

It's said that those closest to the light cast the biggest shadows, meaning that as we move toward the sacred—our soul—we gain power. And if we only see ourselves as good, we've just unconsciously animated a polarity within us and empowered our own "evil"—our shadows—as well. The more we move toward our soul and power, the greater responsibility it becomes to manage our own shadows—especially if we want to transform darkness into light and Fate into Destiny. Therefore, any true spiritual path must integrate the study of this hidden self so that we're better equipped to handle our dark side's potential to do damage when our power increases through our light.

Transformation of the Shadow

So *how* do we manage our darkness? How do we transform our anger, jealousy, greed, fear, hate, discrimination, and desires to self-sabotage? First, we must identify what's in our shadow; we can't work with what we can't see. We can use shadow dancing as an aid in this regard. And once we have that awareness, as I mentioned, we contain the negative quality and then sublimate it into something that isn't harmful.

For example, if you have a bad day running your company and want to verbally abuse all your employees, you take that frustrated energy to the gym and run it out on the treadmill instead of harming your subordinates. I find it useful in dealing with my own shadow to develop a way of ritualistically dialoguing with and transforming its energy. But even then, it can still get the best of me. No doubt, we could all share our stories about our shadow kicking our butt!

Nonetheless, the goal is to continually stand in the middle of our polarities with an eye always on our shadow, and then intend toward the light. This is the true meaning of *holiness*. Unfortunately, all too often, individuals and groups that claim *goodness* as their sole character asset, without admitting their own capacity for evil, fall prey to hubris—an arrogance that has them pointing fingers at everyone else and calling others *evil,* while they fate themselves to an unconscious compulsion to do the very things they tend to vilify and defile. Let's look at another client case that poignantly demonstrates this point. Meet Simon.

Simon: Being Whole, Not Good

Simon was a self-proclaimed right-wing conservative who came to me when he was 28 years old. It was an extraordinary opportunity, as most people in his demographic wouldn't normally be my clients! As I scanned his psyche, I had the overwhelming sense that he'd been raised in a strict home. He confirmed this when he told me that his parents were evangelical Christians and staunch Republicans from Alabama. I could sense that he'd grown up with a rigid belief system birthed from the collective psyche of his fundamentalist community.

Simon said that living in his childhood home was like puritanical boot camp. Reality contained two colors—black and white—and no allowance was made for questioning the interpretations of the Bible as set forth by his family's evangelical church. He came to me after a year of disillusionment in which his clear-cut reality had been shattered when one of their church leaders—a man who fought vehemently against homosexuality, abortion, and infidelity, calling such acts *evil*—had been arrested for having anonymous public sex with a man in a bathroom. What's more, he was married with three kids. This authority figure, my client told me, had personally spearheaded rallies and marches on the local university campus to "save" sinners from the very things that he was doing himself!

Then, later in this same year, Simon's father was found to be having an affair three years strong with another woman, and my client finally began to come to terms with his own molestation as a boy by his Bible-study teacher. Needless to say, this was the beginning of some serious investigation into his faith and what was meaningful for him, and it led him straight into his own personal unconscious, his shadow.

But when I intuitively read Simon, I sensed that he was stepping into a darkness much larger than his own. All that had been repressed and denied by the religious tradition that was fused to his family psyche was *fated* to come out in many destructive forms because it hadn't been consciously acknowledged.

Simon told me more stories—tales of hate mail that members of the church crafted and sent to women in their community who were known to have had abortions, of families supported in the abandonment of their gay children, and of the vilification and labeling as *an agent of evil* of anyone not in agreement with their beliefs.

Yet, because the family and this church couldn't recognize this "evil" as their own, they couldn't engage in the real teachings of Christ: compassion, nonjudgment, acceptance, and forgiveness. These are virtues that are born out of being *whole,* not *good.* Feeling loving kindness for our own evil demands an ongoing, lifelong study of our own darkness and the shadows of the groups we belong to, lest we fall prey to Self Fate.

But once again, it's here, in our most hidden selves, that we also find the buried treasure of the soul. The shadow represents the depths where we find our common humanity. It's the ego that differentiates and divides us so that everything that's denied and projected eventually becomes externalized as an adversary to be fought "out there."

It's the soul that longs for wholeness and calls us—through the mirroring of our dark truths—to the doorstep of integration. The good news is that when we recognize that we're projecting our shadow, we take the first step toward the soul and our true Destiny. Yet, it's still up to us to walk into the darkness and find the light. Paradoxically, *it's when we focus on being whole by befriending our shadow that being good becomes a natural by-product.*

As with shadow dancing, befriending your darker self doesn't mean that you'll act out of your capacity for evil. It means you have a new awareness of yourself, which gives you the choice to not unwittingly harm others through *compulsive* action—a chance to transform Self Fate into Destiny. Befriending your shadow empowers you to *consciously choose* affirming action for all of life instead of being unconsciously driven to react out of a need to protect a cherished and false idea of yourself.

The shadow asks, *Can you love me, own me, and integrate me?* It doesn't ask, *Can you like me?* Clearly, we have qualities that we're just not going to care for, but we can still hold them with compassion and accept them. In fact, loving the shadow is the root of all unconditional love. It's often much easier to cherish our light than our darkness—both in ourselves and in others—but you can only truly care for someone when you love their shadow as well as their light.

I explained these ideas to Simon, rendering him aware of the dynamic that had brought the evangelical house of cards down. And when we spoke again a year later, Simon informed me that his mother and father had saved their marriage through counseling and left the church. My client had also come out about his sexual abuse, and he'd never felt freer to be himself. I was even more amazed when, some time after that, both his father and mother contacted me for a reading! In the end, they'd all transformed Self Fate into Destiny by realizing how polarized and repressed their lives had become in projecting and rejecting their own shadows.

In just the same way that we as individuals project our shadow aspects onto others, groups, nations, and governments project their darker qualities as well. And when they do so, we do it right along with them, pointing fingers, blaming, and even waging war as members of the tribal psyche. This often happens without us ever realizing why we're acting that way, as Simon's story illustrates. It's important to understand this in a nuclear world, because we must collectively comprehend that whatever we reject as an institution, tribe, group, nation, or government can become hostile to us in the same ways that rejected parts of our individual selves can.

When the Rejected Becomes Hostile

Whatever we deny—whether as an individual or a collective—can eventually become hostile toward us and show up as a *fated* circumstance in our environment when we shadow dance. This idea can cause much heated discussion, especially when we apply it to recent world events and the current hostility between nations. This is where we must investigate how we create Fate through collective projection dynamics.

I'm not sure there would be many Americans willing to look at the events of September 11, 2001, as a consequence of the United States not owning its own shadow. Yet the federal government did employ the language of shadow dancing when it called certain parts of the world an *axis of evil* shortly thereafter. Could it be that this horrific event was in fact a collectively *fated* event? In shadow dancing with the Middle East, had the U.S. been mirrored its own capacity for destruction?

Working part-time as a flight attendant during that time, commuting to and based out of Boston, I lost friends in those horrific events, as so many others did. But as of this writing, it's estimated that more than 50,000 people have died at American hands in Afghanistan and Iraq. Didn't these individuals have family and friends, too? Where does it stop?

Perhaps it will end when all nations take responsibility for their own capacity to do harmful damage in the world, reorienting the national self-concept to include the truth that no one is without sin, and therefore, no one may cast a stone at another. My point here isn't to press political buttons, but to illustrate the consequences of shadow projection and Self Fate on the collective level.

The U.S. certainly has a shadow, otherwise Native Americans would still be flourishing and they'd still own most of the land in North America. Historically, there has always been a race of people that conquered and tried to kill off another group and its gods, *but you can't kill a psychic process.* So the more we collectively resist owning the dark parts of what our countries have done, the more our nations are going to shadow dance and be subjected to greater Fate and less Destiny.

The worst Fates—genocide and war—are a shadow dance of the worst kind. Hitler projected his shadow onto the Jews, homosexuals, and anyone else who was a suitable hook, which led to the Holocaust. A more recent example is explored by Immaculée Ilibagiza in her best-selling book, *Left to Tell,* in which she shows how the Hutus' evil and hate projected onto the Tutsis led to the Rwandan genocide.

The impact of the tribal psychic process of projection upon the individual should never be underestimated. No one is born in a vacuum without a connection to the past. But what can we do? We can't take on the whole world, can we? Of course not. This pattern is transformed at the personal level by owning our own shadow, befriending it, and then reworking the psychic patterns of the past into which we were born. As we accomplish this first in our own natures, it then pulses out into our environment. It's in learning to love the inner enemy that we begin to love the outer foes around us.

This is, in essence, transforming Fate into Destiny. Still, we can't alter a culture without first being conscious of its history and contents—and we can't change something inside and outside of us without taking part in it in some way. Therefore, what follows are some questions for your consideration, aimed at helping you assess your participation in shadow dancing at collective levels of consciousness.

It's important to know this because you'll personally reap the consequences of the shadow dancing done by the groups you're a part of, as well as the ways they fate themselves. In other words, you could be creating Self Fate via a community you belong to and identify with as it experiences a Fate Point—and not even know it! Therefore, write down your responses to the following questions in your journal for further reflection:

- What groups do you belong to that expend energy pointing a finger at others, blaming to avoid their own responsibility? How does that affect your personal process of shadow dancing and taking responsibility?

- Are you a part of any organizations that carry a heavy victim consciousness because of things done to them by a sociocultural authority? How does your membership influence your own process of empowerment?

- Are you easily polarized by political discussions? Do you assume a defensive position when someone attacks your country's government or disagrees with its policies? Or do you criticize and attack your government no matter what its actions? What does that highlight regarding the shadow of your nation's leadership and your own shadow dancing?

We've covered the anatomy of our psyche, as well as shadow dancing and the Fate Point. So now we're finally ready to assess the other ways we fate ourselves as we try to keep our psyche and lives stagnant because of our fear of change.

There comes a time when each of us is faced with the fact that Destiny is a verb, not a noun—a journey, not a destination. And we often resist the voice of our Destiny that's calling us forward, instead opting to listen to Fate, which beckons us through fear to stay put. However, remaining where we are will bring us to yet another Fate Point, but this particular one isn't related to not owning negative traits in our shadow. Rather, it's the refusal to birth the creative gold of the soul, and I call it *the dark night of the ego.*

Chapter 12

THE DARK NIGHT OF THE EGO

Transforming Fate into Destiny is the process of becoming your authentic self so that you manifest the mystery of creation, actively embodying purpose, joy, and meaning. You'll never know all of who you are, yet you must live out as much as you can while respecting your own mystery. This is at the root of a *destined* life.

Paradoxically, this is a Fate itself, for it requires that you continue to engage in a process of becoming. Destiny isn't a destination, but the primary way in which you're meant to embody the journey. Although it may direct you to traverse dangerous terrain, take risks, face your fears, and endure loneliness, its intention is that you find your hidden divinity and buried treasure through such perils. Destiny is a dynamic, active, and progressive process that continues to unfold throughout your life. It's activated from the very first breath you take on this planet and doesn't finish until the very last one. It requires you to deliver a unique contribution to this world.

Furthermore, Destiny guides all of us toward something that doesn't come instinctively but must be obtained through conscious effort. This means that we must develop courage and be willing to engage in the constant cycle of losing our self, only to have it reemerge, renewed and reborn—just as we lose the sun every evening as it sets over the horizon, only to rise again with each new dawn.

We can't exclusively hold on to the light of day, what we can see, and what we know. We must also surrender to the darkness of night—the unknown—as a necessary part of our creative and personal renewal. For this is how a new creative aspect of the soul can enter our lives—and it *will* come if we're attentive to our soul's schedule. This is a Divinely designed timeline that your soul agreed to before your incarnation. An important part of it includes waiting for the moments when creative forces within us are finally ready to take their rightful place in our self-concept and be used as the creative allies they were intended to be.

Yet all too often, the soul's intention doesn't jibe with the ego's needs for a secure status quo! It's when we resist this schedule that we'll find ourselves at the threshold of a particular kind of Fate Point, effectively fating ourselves to ask a very crucial question: Do we want a safe life, or an authentic one? So many of us resist this, sensing that the choices we make at these powerful times will be life defining. Indeed, such moments can change the entire trajectory of our existence.

It's human instinct to reach for the familiar, but the soul is here for experience, not security. A life without risk, loss, death, and pain is hardly vitalized. The more we resist the call to adventure, the more we *fate* ourselves to suffering of the worst kind. In such cases, the Universe will often deliver increasingly drastic events until we finally give up the ego's hold on our soul's schedule and allow the next chapter of our purpose—our Destiny—to unfold.

It's at this juncture of resisting our Divine timeline that many of us reach a threshold, often catalyzed by an outer fated event. We've come to know it as *the dark night of the soul.* Yet I always felt that this phrase was a bit of a misnomer because it's the ego, our self-concept, which is actually being set adrift into the unknown. It's here that a part of it must die so that something new from the soul can enter in. And it's the ego that experiences the inherent fear of this change, not the soul. Thus I call this process of entering a transitional space where some new creative aspect of the soul is beginning to birth into your ego structure—which demands that your old self-concept reshape—*the dark night of the ego!*

As I mentioned before, in my personal experience and my work with clients, there's often a fated quality to the events that usher in this dark night of the ego. There could be a job loss, the end of relationship, a crisis of meaning, or an addiction taking over. And whatever it is usually comes to our doorstep as a form of Self Fate because we've been resisting the voice of change—of Destiny—for far too long. This becomes a form of self-sabotage.

Embracing the "In Between"

Nonetheless, whether ushered in by an externalized fated event or not, we'll all encounter the dark night of the ego again and again as part of transforming our Fate into Destiny. The jewel I can offer for when you inevitably encounter the dark night of the ego on your path is this: We need these periods of being "in between." That's essentially what a dark night of the ego is: a space between two identities, a period in which our ego waits to be given new soul coordinates. So why do we have to go through this? I mean, can't we just have our cake and eat it, too? Why can't we have something new enter without having to experience the dark time?

We must understand that *liminality* (a period of being in between) is essential to the revitalization of life and the transformation of Fate into Destiny. It's the bridge without which we couldn't transition from one mode of consciousness to a new one or one way of life to another. Thus, it's essential to midwifing a new creative force into our lives so that it can take root in our identity. However, our first instinct whenever any profound change arrives—especially one that will reshape our lives—is to try to keep things the same. Furthermore, to maintain the status quo, we consult our *old self* for a solution to the problem, when ironically, that's what got us into trouble in the first place!

This is when we must enter into the space between identities in order to source a fresh solution. If we're going to endure, we must animate our interior life and engage in a dialogue with our soul, allowing for something new to be born. For as we step into a liminal space, going back to the old self will only bring more problems and inevitably *fate* us to more oh-so-fun Divine interventions that feel like a whack with a two-by-four!

From here, if we can learn to embrace the unknown in this groundless state, we can open up to a new vision and the unlived potential within us that couldn't be housed in the old life. Liminality can be a dark place, a void in which we must rely on the eyes of our soul to see in the darkness. Once we do this and respect our own mystery, we see a new day dawning.

Navigation of the unknown requires using our tools to transform Fate into Destiny: acceptance, authentic choice, surrender, prayer, and the Law of Attraction—all of which allow for the optimal openness to Divine design. We must embrace the fact that this dark state of chaos is the genesis of all things new. Transforming Fate into Destiny becomes very urgent within this void—in fact, it's where we must do the most work. And although our tools are helpful, we'll need something else, too: a technique of discernment that helps us confront our fears.

I've come to realize that during the dark night of the ego, it's as if Fate and Destiny speak to us through two distinct voices. We must be able to tell the difference between the two, and then how we respond to them becomes the measure of whether we *fate* or *destine* ourselves.

Throughout this section, you've been learning that Self Fate relates greatly to how you create your own Fate, often by resisting the new creative forces surfacing within you that will enact change in your life. And although the exercises in the following chapter are mostly applicable to transforming Self Fate into Destiny, use the examples to put into practice *everything* this book has taught you thus far.

CHAPTER 13

THE VOICE OF FATE VS. THE VOICE OF DESTINY

While we're in the dark night of the ego, we're each greeted by two competing voices: that of Fate (ego) and that of Destiny (soul). The former speaks through your fears, your past, your wounds, and the collective *they* that you worry about when you make decisions. The latter communicates through your intuition, dreams, synchronicity, Divine intervention, and the regrets that tug at your soul. Both continually compete to guide the choices you make during this vital time.

At the crossroads of the dark night of the ego, these two voices essentially ask, *Will you choose based on your fear or your highest potential?* Decisions made from anxiety are actions of Self Fate because they *fate* us to events and circumstances designed to make us face what we're afraid of. Thus, Self Fate choices are usually made to stave off survival worries or to keep the past alive, instead of letting our present vibrate anew with unknown possibilities.

Decisions made out of unknown possibility, however, are ones of Destiny; they lead to the actualization of your highest potential. They demand trust, risk, letting go of the past, being present, and manifesting the best of what's inside of you without making any apologies. Destiny choices demand an allegiance to the soul.

Discerning which impulse you allow to guide your life can be tricky, but it's essential. What follows is an example of how each voice might speak to you during the dark night of the ego. As you read the scenarios, imagine yourself surrounded by each influence, then begin to recognize which voice you listen to most often. In fact, it would be empowering to spend some time discerning which one you're giving allegiance to in the decisions you make—not only during the dark night of the ego, but every day.

Starting Over

- **Voice of Fate:** "You can't go back to college for a new career—you're too old. Not to mention, what would everyone think of you on campus? How would you afford it?"

- **Voice of Destiny:** "It's never to late to learn something new. Think of how exciting it would be to attend class again! Imagine how exhilarated you'd be as you're surrounded by young minds, full of fresh ideas. You can make the money work out somehow. If it's meant to be, nothing can stop you!"

Your Marriage

- **Voice of Fate:** "You can't leave this marriage. How will you find someone else at your age? And what will your kids think? Okay, so your husband isn't the most emotionally available man, but hey, he takes care of the mortgage! Why on earth would you want to give up that security? And so what if you haven't had sex in two years? Most people don't after they turn 50 anyway."

- **Voice of Destiny:** "Get out of this marriage now, girlfriend! You can make it on your own. There are tons of good-looking hotties out there interested in women your age—there are gentlemen ready for a spiritual partnership! You can't afford to sell your soul for the mortgage anymore. Your kids will be better off if you heal the family psyche by breaking this legacy of codependency. And don't you know that sex for women just begins to flower after 50?"

Your Job

- **Voice of Fate:** "You can't leave this job. So what if you're constantly stressed and unhappy, have ulcers, and can't sleep because of it. You've been here for 20 years. What the hell else are you gonna do? And what about your pension and retirement? It's too late to go start a business of your own, so get over that pipe dream."

- **Voice of Destiny:** "Have you not heard me talking to you through your body? This job is killing you! You've been here for 20 years, and come on now, you're only 45—there's so much more you could do and pursue. What about your dream of opening a small shop, selling imported cheese and wine? You know so much about the subject and are so passionate about it—how could it not work? Take the early retirement package and go for it!"

Your Creative Idea

- **Voice of Fate:** "Look, you can't be the next Martha Stewart, so why bother going forward with your idea for a vegetarian cooking show? Get over yourself, Betty Crocker! If you can't be the best in your field, then why bother. You should just stop with this nonsense that you have any sort of original ideas. Trust me—it's all been done before."

- **Voice of Destiny:** "You have something unique that you can offer through a vegetarian cooking show. You have to do this! Of course you won't be the next Martha Stewart—you'll be *you!* Just because you might not be the most famous person in your field doesn't mean that you don't have something wonderful to contribute to others. And you'll undoubtedly contribute something special. It hasn't all been done before because only you can do it *your* way—and that will shine out into the world."

Love

- **Voice of Fate:** "What on earth are you thinking?! The last time you took a risk in love, you got hurt. You know that you only draw in women who abandon you. What do you think you're doing by opening up your heart again? Come on, she'll only break up with you for someone else who's better looking and has more money . . . just the way they all have."

- **Voice of Destiny:** "Yes, you've had some painful experiences in your past, but you've grown so much! This woman really likes you, so you should give her—and yourself—a chance to try again. You know that you have nothing to fear now because you've learned not to abandon yourself. There's a good chance this relationship could mirror that back to you! How will you know if you don't try? This is the present moment of all possibility. Don't you want to feel alive? Destiny is risk, so take it and open your heart."

Now, I could continue with examples of these two viewpoints for pages on end, but I think that I've given you enough to understand how they speak to you. Essentially, your highest potential is the voice of Destiny; it almost always demands that you risk and sacrifice for the unknown. Living in alignment with it is often full of surprises—some joyful, some painful—but when you embrace this path, you'll know you're alive! When you can say to yourself, *I never thought I would* ____________, what fills that blank space is your Destiny.

This voice can also demand that you come to terms with something. For example, it might whisper in your ear, *You know that you're addicted to your entitlement as a victim and are a huge narcissist, don't you? Are you ready to deal with that?* Or it might say, *You realize that your son is addicted to drugs. Are you ready to confront him?* And perhaps you'll hear, *You know that your spouse is having an affair. Are you ready to finally admit and address it?* In other words, coming to terms with something also transforms Self Fate into Destiny.

I'd like to share another case where someone found himself in the dark night of the ego and then had to choose which voice to listen to. His first decision was to listen to Fate, which brought a self-fated event into his life. It was only when he chose to heed the voice of Destiny that he began to heal. This story will resonate with most of us because we'll all encounter a situation where the creativity of our soul begins to knock on the door of our ego. And if we don't invite this part of us into the ego as a noble guest, we'll also meet Fate. With that said, I'd like you to meet Patrick.

The Soul's Emerging Needs

Patrick's story embodies one of the most important things to remember about Self Fate, the process of fating ourselves, and how to transform that into Destiny. We must see the events of our lives symbolically so that when something happens to us, we first ask ourselves, *Why did this occur, and what does it mean? What fragments of myself that I need to awaken to are being mirrored through this event?*

Things take place every day, and on the surface they appear to have no cause. Yet if they're perceived symbolically, the meaning may be readily apparent. Then we see components of our Self Fate being mirrored back to us. Our inner and outer worlds work in tandem to ensure that we recognize the creative force in us that's begging to be expressed. Otherwise, we think that events are just coming at us, and we're victims of circumstance rather than participants in our soul's schedule.

Time and time again, I've had clients ask for help in decoding the events of their lives, understanding why they feel the way they do, and figuring out what lesson is being delivered through their challenges. Patrick was no exception when he came to me at age 40 for a reading. He sought me out because he was in a deep depression and felt that his job as recruiter for a New York City corporation was going to kill him. As I do with all my clients, I read his psyche before our session and picked up on a strong block regarding a new force emerging into his life—the creative artist within him.

I intuited that he came from a military family that was focused on duty and responsibility. As you can imagine, creativity never made it onto the list of what men in this family were encouraged to develop! But you can't stop the soul, and Patrick's latent artistic side was ready to come out and create. By the time we met, this force had been fighting with his resistant ego for two years, and much of his psychic energy was exhausted.

Tired and unhappy, Patrick had officially entered a *creative depression.* The ego's hold over his self-concept had to weaken enough so that his creative impulses could get through to him as a valid force. The time had come in his Divine timeline to awaken and incarnate this part of his soul. To be sure, he'd need to fuse his artistic agency with the more fully developed practical side of his nature, but I could sense that his current life would be unable to house that fusion. Leaving his job was imminent and necessary to his psychic survival.

I also sensed that if Patrick didn't listen to his soul and let it set his course, he'd probably suffer from more severe consequences that would manifest as health issues. He confirmed that he'd been daydreaming about moving from New York to Santa Fe, where he could take a break and explore his next steps. We concluded the session, and my client seemed excited about the new options we'd discussed for his future.

But a year later, after being hospitalized for severe depression and ulcers, Patrick contacted me for a second reading. He hadn't changed a thing. In fact, he'd stayed at his job only to be given even more responsibility with little financial compensation. Increasingly bitter and angry, he was projecting much of his unhappiness onto New York City and the people there. Sensing that the situation was deteriorating, I asked him why he hadn't made any new choices. *Why hadn't he listened to the voice of Destiny, instead opting for the voice of Fate? Why had he chosen to fate himself in such ways?*

"I wanted to save more money before making the leap," Patrick explained, adding that his parents had warned him against the venture altogether. I then realized that his ego had been hijacked by external forces, leaving him unable to take the risk of *letting the soul decide*. Instead, he'd opted for the Fate of a major health issue.

Six months later, Patrick finally acted. He quit his job and moved to Santa Fe to explore his artistic side.

Within two years, then age 43, he was flourishing as a landscaper and owned his own company. This new work allowed him to create, be outside, and use the skills he'd gained in the corporate world. He was ulcer free and no longer depressed. Through incorporating his inner creative needs into a functional dialogue with his practical entrepreneurial side, landscaping had become the perfect manifestation of Destiny out of his Fate. The transformation was complete, setting him on a new course in life.

There comes a time in all of our lives when the soul is ready to introduce a new facet of our Cosmic Contract, and we must animate an unfamiliar aspect of our identity. It's at this point that Fate and Destiny begin to dance anew. Your *power of choice* is what determines which pattern you find yourself in—that of Destiny or Fate.

But making choices, as you've learned, can be complex business and is only the beginning. For example, let's say you're listening to the voice of Destiny and making choices accordingly. You feel as though you've been recognizing and owning your soul's new emerging needs, but you still find that fated events keep befalling you right, left, and center! So you wonder, *Now what, Robert?*

Well, I'm glad you asked, because there are a few more things to consider and weave into the complexities of transforming Self Fate into Destiny. Namely, we must address and discern when we're looking at a *creative obstacle* or a *fated redirection* in the events that come our way. In other words, how do we know when we're on the right track and must persevere through a rough patch, or when we're off course and need to abandon ship?

To answer these questions, we must remember to check in with our inner authority and cultural spells, and beyond that see what's left in the equation—for that will determine whether we stay on a given path that's our *authentic passion*. But before we can speak about that subject, let's briefly define our terms.

Creative Obstacles and Fated Redirections

Having a sense of how Fate and Destiny speak to us as distinct voices is key, but what about the obstacles that seem to keep blocking our way, especially when we feel that we *are* making choices guided by the voice of Destiny? It's important to realize and accept that obstacles in life are actually *part* of the destined path! I can't tell you how many clients have complained that they're taking the risks and listening to the voice of Destiny, yet it still seems that nothing is going their way.

I like to use the following analogy when addressing this issue: Imagine that our experience on this planet is like signing up to run a hurdle race. Before your soul came here, it knew that there would be obstacles (hurdles) in this life (race) that would have to be surmounted again and again. So you get up to the starting line and the gun fires (you're born), and you start running the race (you begin your life). And what do you know—you come up to your first hurdle (life obstacle)!

You begrudgingly hop over it, life goes on, and you continue down the track. And guess what, you arrive at another hurdle. Now you're more than mildly annoyed. Still, you hop over it and continue on again, complaining to yourself, *Someone's gonna get it! I mean, who keeps putting these hurdles [obstacles] on the track [your path]?*

As you keep running, you round the first corner and dang it—another hurdle! Now you're frustrated and angry, and you plop yourself down on the track, screaming, "What's going on?! Who keeps putting these hurdles in my way?" Finally, the person in charge of the race (God) comes up to you. "What's wrong with you?" God asks. "Don't you remember that you signed up for the *hurdle* race?"

This story might make you laugh. (I hope it does!) We've all sat down on the track of life because we came across an obstacle. I've done it before, and I know I'll do it again. It's only human—it's natural to get frustrated. Still, it's also worthwhile to investigate the nature of the challenges that befall us on our journey of Destiny. In fact, understanding what blocks our path is the only way we'll overcome it.

Some difficulties arise from our own unconsciousness showing up as Self Fate—we've covered that. Yet, sometimes stumbling blocks are actually *fated redirection,* arriving at just the right time to push us off the wrong path and onto the right one for our life's purpose. These obstacles show up as hurdles that are simply too high for us to jump over and continue in the same race. They force us to run a different course with challenges that we can overcome.

Other times, obstructions arrive to challenge us to develop our character in ways that allow our soul to surface, or they may show up as wounds that catalyze the expansion of our awareness through our healing. These are *creative obstacles,* because they form new openings in our consciousness. They're the hurdles that we can surmount and clear, but only through our best selves stepping forward.

How can we recognize the difference between a *fated redirection* and a *creative obstacle?* Let's investigate this and then look at a story that demonstrates the importance of making the distinction.

Knowing Your Passion

Before you can begin to discern the difference between a fated redirection and creative obstacle, you must take an honest look at the path you're on—the choices that are bringing one or the other to your doorstep. Most notably, you must go inside and sense your true intentions, asking yourself, *Am I pursuing something because of outer goals or for the promise of the accolades it might bring me—fame, money, status, acceptance, respect, a relationship, or admiration? Or am I on this path because of inner goals and an internal calling that beckons me—that is, because I feel passionate?*

Passion is often very misunderstood in our culture, usually relegated to a feeling that becomes our impulsive undoing. We've all heard of "crimes of passion," actions taken in an emotionally charged state without intellectual awareness of the consequences. This is *not* what I mean by the word. In fact, these should really be called "crimes of compulsion"!

Authentic passion is an impulse of the soul that flows into your feelings as an awareness that you *adore* doing something. Many clients ask me what they should pursue in life, to which I often reply, "What do you love to do?" They usually say something such as *helping others, working with kids, teaching, or travel.* I tell them that those are threads of passion that are meant to be embodied in their purpose, but their answers are much too vague to be useful.

To get a sense of what your passion is, try to imagine what would get you out of bed in the morning with a spring in your step! What *really* excites you? Passion is a intuitive spark from the soul that seeks to ignite your life through your creative expression—without caring what others think. It serves as guidance about what you need to focus your attention and resources on in order to feel alive.

And once you've identified what could be a passion, you must ascertain if it's coming from within you or if it's something your culture has made you long for—a cultural spell. For example, many people are drawn to the bright lights of Hollywood not because they're *passionate* about acting, but because they want to feel *special.* That's an experience never afforded them by their family or their culture, and their longing is masquerading as passion. Similarly, many people enter the healing arts and claim it as a passion when their unconscious agenda has more to do with being praised for exceptional abilities than with healing others.

By now you're probably wondering, *Robert, what does all this have to do with discerning the difference between fated redirection and creative obstacles?* In a word, everything! If you're on a path that lacks connection to authentic passion, you'll be sent fated redirections by the Universe because what you're doing isn't part of your life's purpose. This guidance can arrive in innumerable ways, most often manifesting as depression, certain "accidents" that keep you from progressing, financial disasters, physical injuries or illness, relationships ending, infidelity, exhaustion, frustration, and failure.

Therefore, knowing your passion becomes the decisive factor in whether you experience obstacles designed as fated redirections. And to know what you truly love, you must enter into dialogue with your shadow. You have to assess what possible options your ego is filtering out and repressing because they won't make you tons of money, give you recognition, or fit in with other people's expectations or because they might embarrass you. Authentic passion is intuitive guidance at its finest, but it can't lead you if you don't let it through. Thus it needs *inner authority* and *soul-esteem* in order to surface.

One place we can look for clues to our true calling is childhood. I believe that as kids, before societal and parental conditioning had taken root, we were more in touch with what we wanted, most often evidenced in our dreams of what we wanted to become when we grew up. Not that what we picked needs to be taken literally, but it can most definitely be embraced symbolically! When you were young, what did you say when someone asked you, *What do you want to be when you grow up?*

For example, I wanted to be a teacher and an artist when I was a child, and symbolically that's what I've become, in part. It's exactly what I discovered when I was looking for my authentic passion: I love to teach through the creativity of storytelling and performing on stage.

Identifying Your Passions

Ask yourself these questions about your current activities and pursuits. The more times you answer yes, the more likely it is that you've identified a passion.

- Do you dream about it?
- Do you get excited when you think about doing it?
- Do you lose track of time when you're engaged in it?
- Do you feel energized during and after this activity, rather than tired?
- Do you do it really well?
- Do you feel empowered when doing it?
- Do other people comment on how well you're doing and how happy you seem to be?

Journal about this exercise, and note the passions—or lack thereof—in your life. Then allow yourself to think about what other options you may not have considered yet as valid keys to your Destiny and why that is.

Mystical Stamina

Identifying your authentic passion will change certain dynamics on your life path of Destiny. It won't make things any easier, but instead of fated redirection (interventions sent to bring you back into harmony with your Cosmic Contract and purpose), you'll be sent *creative obstacles.* These are continual challenges designed not to take you off the path but to build up greater strength for the next phase of the journey. They, too, can show up in innumerable ways, but instead of redirecting you, they're all intended to build *mystical stamina*. This is the capacity to *keep the faith* during a trial while building soulful endurance.

If you're in touch with your true passion, a creative obstacle is meant to help you bring it out more effectively in the world. Often, the issue at hand when such a challenge arrives is how your ego functions as an interface for the soul. For example, let's say that you're a talented and soulful singer, *destined* to make it big. You sing about spirituality and the human experience—soul songs. Your music isn't produced for mass consumption just to make a fast buck, and it transforms people's lives.

You know that you're meant to do this—to be a singer—but you've spent the last ten years playing at local coffeehouses and clubs, and you still haven't been discovered or caught a break. You've been financially challenged every step of the way, you've moved to various cities that you thought would help you make the necessary connections, and you've been through numerous humiliating experiences. All of this has inspired even more soul songs. Still, you're fed up and cry out to the gods, *Enough is enough!*

Are you on the wrong path? Absolutely not. But before the Universe can empower you with a new level of success, time must season you with creative obstacles. These challenges humble your ego so that when you finally do become successful—your Destiny—you'll be strong enough not to suffer from ego inflation. That, in turn, will allow you to create as you were meant to, even when the money and success arrive. The humble wiring of your ego will remain intact, allowing your soul to inform the process of living and creating out of your passion, even when you no longer have the difficult circumstances to draw from.

So let's ground these ideas in a couple of client cases. This first example shows how fated redirections continued to show up for one man, but he just couldn't listen—which led to him fating himself to bankruptcy. The second story relates to another person's resistance to creative obstacles as a lifelong process. Meet Joe and Phyllis.

A Fated Redirection

Joe initially came to me when a business he'd started with his wife was on the verge of collapse. The couple had been in jobs that they couldn't stand and finally decided to venture out on their own by creating a company that sold imported cabinetry from Europe.

Together they pooled all their savings and resources to get things off the ground, and they opened up a small showroom in Boston. A year into their business, however, signs of trouble began to surface. Although they'd been given some exposure through TV and other forms of media, their offerings weren't catching on. This began to bring out the underlying dysfunction of their marriage as well.

When I read Joe, I perceived that the whole of his enterprise was built on a faulty foundation. I could sense that not only was his partner, his wife, not suitable emotionally to run a company with him—he also wasn't in touch with his authentic passion. He confirmed that all he felt was stress, and he didn't even know what the word *passion* meant anymore. Furthermore, he was now deeply in debt, and things had gotten quite dire.

He and his wife had been forced to move out of the home they owned because the bank had foreclosed on it, and they were living illegally in a room within the commercial space that housed their cabinet showroom. They were set to be evicted from there, too, because of owing back rent for a year! Joe told me that if he were out of debt, he'd actually leave his marriage because he'd realized the ways his wife emotionally manipulated him. Then he said, "I just don't know what to do, Robert. I mean, how do we know whether our lack of success is due to a need of further perseverance or if we're simply on the wrong track altogether?"

This question held the key to his clarity. I replied, "Joe, you need to take a look at the reality of things here. You're nearly bankrupt, you've lost equity in the home you owned, you're illegally living in a commercial space, and you're about to become homeless. And in your heart, you know that you need to get out of your marriage." I pressed him further and asked, "What will it take to make you see things clearly? What more Fate must arrive to wake you up?"

When we ended the session, I knew that Joe had yet to hit bottom. Sadly, he couldn't absorb the reality of what life was showing him so clearly. Months later, he contacted me to say that I was accurate: Life had clearly been sending him a fated redirection. He was eventually forced to declare bankruptcy. He divorced his wife and had to move in with his brother once he was evicted from his showroom space. He lost it all in the end, but I encouraged him to see it as a significant gain, for he was finally free to get in touch with his passion and resurrect himself through it.

This story does, however, point to what we each need to do in navigating our fated redirections. We must look with unflinching honesty at our situation and assess whether we're motivated to keep going by passion or fear. Joe was afraid not only of failure, but also of the responsibility that loomed ominously in front of him—that of dismantling an old life.

Creative Obstacles

If authentic passion is the engine driving our life, then we're most likely standing in front of a creative obstacle, not a fated redirection (although we resist those, too). The Universe will always present us with challenges; they're part of a destined path. Yet I've found that many people falsely believe that once they're on a path they feel is purposeful, they should no longer suffer any hardships—especially if their journey is one of healing service. If only that were true! The next story involves delivering this truth—with difficulty. This client was not too happy about the nature of Destiny and creative obstacles.

Phyllis was in her 50s and was just leaving her career as a nurse when she contacted me. As I read her psyche, I picked up that she'd been badly abused as a child and had lived a very rough life as an adult. While practicing nursing, she'd discovered that she was a healer. She'd come to me to confirm her intuition that it was time for her to retire from nursing and begin a private healing practice.

I intuited that she was indeed a healer, and her ability was connected to her pattern of being a *wounded* healer. This meant that her soul had chosen a very damaging life so that she might mend her own injuries and then use the wisdom gained to aid others. Although I sensed that she should, indeed, begin a healing practice, I also understood that she had an overinflated idea of how it would unfold. I could tell that she'd created a fantasy of a new vocation where no hardships would befall her ever again.

My intuition was confirmed when Phyllis said, "I've had a hard life, but I've reached a point where no obstacles will stop me anymore. Finally, I can begin healing others."

As gently as I could, I explained that the wounded-healer pattern she carried meant that the progress she'd made in this lifetime had initiated her into her calling. As a requirement of helping people the way she was meant to, other trials and initiations would always be waiting. I said, "Those of us called to be in this field are continually tending to ourselves and discovering new wounds that we didn't know were there. When you're working as a wounded healer, you can only assist others by virtue of that which you've had to overcome."

Phyllis didn't take the news so well. She believed that because of the suffering she'd already endured, she was entitled to be a successful healer who would endure no more pain.

This reading reminded me that many people think of Destiny as a noun—as something we're assigned or given—when really it's more like a verb—something we must work for and with. It also isn't painless, although the Fate we create in resisting it is *painful.*

Creative obstacles will never stop showing up—ever! It's better to focus on how to use them as lessons of empowerment. So how can you do that? You implement the tools from earlier in this book—acceptance, authentic choice, surrender, prayer, and the Law of Attraction—not by doing nothing. In fact, sometimes you need to keep trying and overcoming challenges until you're finally up that damn mountain! When you engage the tool of ***prayer,*** you don't ask for the mountain to be taken away, because the act of climbing it is building something in you that will be crucial for the next phase of the journey. Instead, you pray for help up the mountain, and then ***accept*** however assistance shows up.

Every prayer is answered, without exception, but you must employ acute awareness in perceiving the response. Realize that you may simply be told to make the most of this difficult circumstance and keep on livin'!

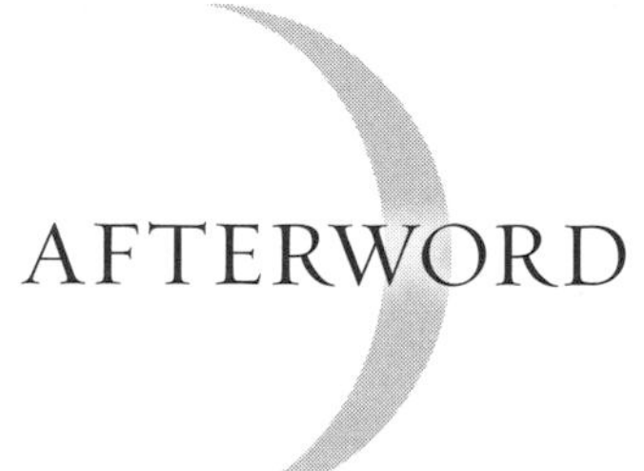

AFTERWORD

God grant us the serenity to accept the things we cannot change, courage to change the things we can, and wisdom to know the difference.
— The Serenity Prayer, by Reinhold Niebuhr

In today's high-speed world, many books on self-help and spirituality like to offer a formula that needs to be put in place only once in order to change your life and help you find your purpose. That's it, now you're done, goal achieved! I want you to understand something very important about *this* book: Transforming your Fate into Destiny must be embraced as a continuing process, not a one-time event. It's a lifetime contract and commitment—as is your purpose.

There will always be a part of us that remains a mystery. We must respect it as ultimately unknowable, yet paradoxically, we must make efforts to fully discover it! For by searching for the unknown, we discover our soul and our gods. Thus, I find myself wondering how I can bring to a close the subject of Fate and Destiny—one that I could write volumes on and never be finished! Full of its own mystery, this subject has stalked me, haunted me, fascinated me, vitalized me, terrified me, and loved me my whole life, and I know it always will.

It's important, then, for me to emphasize that the terrain of this book is one I will walk every day, just like you. I've always felt that no one can authentically teach others anything that they haven't experienced themselves to some degree. And believe me, I've had my share of Mortal Fate and Self Fate to transform into Destiny in this lifetime.

The voices of Fate and Destiny call to me, and they're beckoning you, too. Dialoguing with our soul is an ongoing discipline and spiritual path. We must take risks, be courageous, and realize that each time we hear them, we're being asked to enter the sacred space of our interior. In doing so, we must walk into our soul each time with newfound humility and then have an attitude of openness toward what we find.

Furthermore, whenever we venture within ourselves, it will be a different experience as we uncover new paths in our consciousness. This allows us to stay present to the mystery of who we are. Only then can we revitalize our lives and move through our dark nights of the ego with poise.

I hope that you can turn to this book for years to come and continue to use it as a guide in the process of actualizing your unique purpose in this lifetime. And let there be no doubt that you have a specific mission and grace to deliver to the world. Others—myself included—are counting on you to animate your goodness and compassion on our behalf so that we, too, can be lifted higher toward our reason for being.

Your Fate will continue to lead you toward your purpose, your Destiny. And only you can bring forth the particular grace you must embody and live out in this world. It's my wish that you be empowered by this book to:

- Accept what you can't change, and discern and put energy into the things you can.

- Recognize your Mortal Fate as a guide toward your purpose, rather than fearing it as a limitation that keeps you from achieving your Destiny.

- Befriend your shadow so that you can wield your light, arresting Self Fate in its tracks as you own your buried treasures and become compassionate toward your inner and outer enemies.

- Embrace each dark night of the ego as a new opportunity for an unknown creative aspect of your soul to be incarnated into your life.

- Listen more to the voice of Destiny and less to the voice of Fate.

- Be able to identify your creative obstacles and fated redirections.

- Live from your passion and soul.

For the rest of my life, I'll be struggling right along with you to honor my agreements with Fate and Destiny.

Fate will ask me, "Robert, what will you do with what I've given you?" And I know that how I answer will be my Destiny. For me, this can often be a painful responsibility to acknowledge and assume, as I am sure it will be for you. But it can also be the source of magic and joy for all of us.

The intention of the soul is to walk this creative path of transforming challenges into gifts. It's reassuring to know that we have numerous helpers on the path with us: acceptance, choice, surrender, prayer, and the Law of Attraction. What do you say—shall we walk this path together and remember that our ultimate Destiny is to offer service and companionship to one another? In that regard, may this book be my extension of assistance to you, an invitation to make the journey of transforming Fate into Destiny hand in hand.

It's a trip well worth the travel. And my soul tells me that we mustn't wait another day to embark on this path, for there's much Fate to transform in this world. I hope you'll take my hand and remain by my side throughout the adventure.

Namaste,
Robert

ACKNOWLEDGMENTS

The birth of this book wouldn't have been possible without so many amazing, generous people who gave support in the ways only they could. In that regard, I must first thank Caroline Myss. Without you, Caroline, this book simply would never have happened. I'll never forget your belief in me, constant support, love, kicks in the ass when needed, and crazy generosity. Your counsel resurrected me many times when I thought I couldn't continue with this project. You've taught me so much about dialoguing with my soul over the years and have been the best mentor I could have asked the gods to send me. Thank you from my soul. I'm indebted to you beyond measure.

I wish to also thank everyone at CMED: David Smith, my agent and friend—the book brought out the best in both of us and for that I am so grateful; you're like a brother to me. Cindy Funfsinn, thanks for so many fun memories and for reminding me that forgiveness can always bring a new beginning if you let it. Jill Angelo, my special angel who always believed in my potential and never let me forget it: Thanks for your cards, love, and support—I love you. Lynn Charland, your Amazonian spirit and perspective always made me feel vitalized and empowered!

I was graced by the opportunity to work with two wonderful editors on this book. Thanks to Amy Oscar. You helped so much with the first vision of the book as you worked your line-editing magic. And thanks to Angela Hynes—not only did I get a great editor with you, but a new friend. You were invaluable to this project and brought the soul of this book to the earth. You allowed my voice to remain intact yet added new dimension and polish to my words. You're amazing!

A special thanks to my new Hay House family. Ron Tillinghast, you spotted me in the crowd and got this whole thing rolling, you crazy man, you. Louise Hay, in synchronicity you offered me the wisest counsel on how to allow this book to evolve and change; thank you for your faith in me. Jill Kramer, thank you for your patience while I figured out what the heck I was doing, and for believing in me all the way up to the final version! Jessica Kelley, thank you for being compassionate enough to give me your editorial vision straight up; this book wouldn't have found its voice without your honesty. Nancy Levin, thanks for making me smile, you goddess, you. And thanks to Diane Ray of Hay House Radio. Christy Salinas—you're too fun! Thanks to Julie Davison for an amazing cover and to Reid Tracy for giving me a chance.

Last but not least of my Hay House family, thanks to my new big sister, Colette Baron-Reid—you'll never know how much I adore you and what your support meant to me at such a vulnerable time. You were unbelievably generous with your encouragement and belief in my message. I'm beyond grateful that you're in my life, knowing our journey together has only just begun! And to my new big brother, John Holland, your genuine unconditional support was also a huge gift. I'm blessed to have you as a friend and colleague.

To my dear late friend Jenny Peterson: Jenny, I know you were around me the whole time I wrote this, encouraging me and supporting me just as you did when you were alive in this world. I'll always miss you and feel your loss here until we meet again. I love you. Thanks to the Petersons for letting me openly honor Jenny as an integral part of this book.

To my late father, thank you for everything you did for me and for honoring our contract by giving me the Fate that I could later transform into Destiny. You're always in my heart, and I love you.

To my amazing mom, you represent what Destiny means to me in every sense of the word. You taught me that we can resurrect from our crucifixions and ascend to a new life. You're the most amazing human being I know. I love you.

To my brother Matt, your help on my Website was invaluable. You're my dearest soul mate. We've had much Fate to transform into Destiny together in this lifetime and never once left the sacredness, bond, and love of our brotherhood. I love you more than words can say, and always will. Thank you for being in my Cosmic Contract as my brother—one of the greatest gifts this lifetime. And thanks to your lovely wife, Meredith; my beautiful niece, Leslie; and my nephew, Jimmy, for reminding me of what matters. Dad is surely proud.

Thanks to my dear circle of friends: David Perrott, who gave me some of my first lessons in vocabulary usage and grammar, often much to my chagrin! In many ways, you were my first editor, but most important, you continue to teach me what best friends are all about and remind me that "bugs" may be the one thing in this life that are truly forever. To Victoria Drake, my depth psychological muse who played Hermes to me as I descended into the shadows while writing this book: Thanks for your late-night talks and always inspiring me with new perspectives. Paul Stovall, your music still feeds my soul and makes me sing. Jennifer Watkins, my fellow seeker and friend, I'm so grateful for our connection. Kat Truman, our experience helped midwife me into the intuitive arts again. Cara Detlefsen, thanks for encouraging me to take those first steps all those years ago that led to this book—who would have thought? You are always in my heart. Thanks to Dan Simpson for making me smile and being my partner in crime ever since college. Ben Dykes, thanks for asking me to get a Tarot reading from you all those years ago.

You played such an important part in my purpose—thank you for the passion and generosity you brought forward as my first spiritual director.

I'd also like to thank those who have influenced my work immensely, both the living and those who have passed on: Erin Sullivan, Liz Greene, Alice O. Howell, Dane Rudhyar, Joseph Campbell, Carl Jung, Michael Meade, Edgar Cayce, Wayne Dyer, James Hillman, Richard Tarnas, Plato, Virgil, Hesiod, and Rumi. A part of each of you is found within these pages.

Last, I must thank the Guides, Angels, and Souls that are always around me acting as part of my own Team. Without your support and Divine interventions, I couldn't have made it this far in life—this I know. Thanks to the unnameable creative force, the Universe, and the gods that love me even when I'm fooled into not loving myself.

And thanks to the Being that called me to Her presence years ago, officially launching me on the quest to understand the paradox of Fate and Destiny as being the same force in the end, that I am both Fated and free, that my Fate is also my Destiny. I hope I have honored our encounter through the writing of this book. I offer you my deepest gratitude for having summoned me to you. I know that I'll see you again when my final Fate comes for me—which I hope ain't too soon!

BIBLIOGRAPHY

These are some of the books that have influenced me greatly, specifically when it comes to many of the ideas I have presented in this book:

Bly, Robert. *A Little Book on the Human Shadow.* San Francisco. Harper & Row, 1988.

Eadie, Betty J. *Embraced by the Light.* New York. Bantam Books, 1994.

Greene, Liz. *The Astrology of Fate.* York Beach, Maine. Samuel Weiser, Inc, 1984.

Hicks, Esther and Jerry. *The Amazing Power of Deliberate Intent.* Carlsbad, California. Hay House, Inc., 2006.

Howell, Alice O. *Jungian Synchronicity in Astrological Signs and Ages.* Wheaton, Illinois. Quest Books, 1990.

Johnson, Robert. *Owning Your Own Shadow.* San Francisco. Harper, 1993.

Myss, Caroline. *Sacred Contracts.* New York. Harmony Books, 2001.

———. *Invisible Acts of Power.* New York. Free Press, 2004.

Schwartz, Robert. *Courageous Souls.* Ashland, Oregon. Whispering Winds Press, 2007.

Sullivan, Erin. *The Astrology of Midlife and Aging.* New York. Tarcher/Penguin, 2005.

———. *Saturn in Transit.* York Beach, Maine. Samuel Wiser, Inc, 2000.

Williamson, Marianne. *Illuminata.* New York. Riverhead Books, 1994.

ABOUT THE AUTHOR

Robert Ohotto is a writer, teacher, intuitive consultant, and practicing professional astrologer based in Chicago. He has a diverse background of study in mythology, Christian mysticism, Kabbalah, Jungian psychology, Eastern philosophy, and Western Hermetic teachings.

An energetic and engaging speaker, Robert is highly sought after worldwide for his integrative lectures and his intuitive and astrological consultations. For more than 15 years, he's been a pioneer and new voice within the field of intuitive astrology and human consciousness.

Robert is also an up-and-coming radio and television personality and writes articles on consciousness for various Websites and publications. For three years, he taught with world-renowned medical intuitive Caroline Myss at her Caroline Myss Education (CMED) Institute in Chicago. He's currently founding his own institute of intuitive and astrological studies.

For more information on Robert's work and lecture schedule visit him at his popular Website: **www.ohotto.com**.

We hope you enjoyed this Hay House book. If you'd like to receive a free catalog featuring additional Hay House books and products, or if you'd like information about the Hay Foundation, please contact:

Hay House, Inc.
P.O. Box 5100
Carlsbad, CA 92018-5100

(760) 431-7695 or **(800) 654-5126**
(760) 431-6948 (fax) or **(800) 650-5115 (fax)**
www.hayhouse.com® • www.hayfoundation.org

Published and distributed in Australia by: Hay House Australia Pty. Ltd., 18/36 Ralph St., Alexandria NSW 2015 • *Phone:* 612-9669-4299 *Fax:* 612-9669-4144 • www.hayhouse.com.au

Published and distributed in the United Kingdom by: Hay House UK, Ltd., 292B Kensal Rd., London W10 5BE • *Phone:* 44-20-8962-1230 • *Fax:* 44-20-8962-1239 • www.hayhouse.co.uk

Published and distributed in the Republic of South Africa by: Hay House SA (Pty), Ltd., P.O. Box 990, Witkoppen 2068 • *Phone/Fax:* 27-11-467-8904 • orders@psdprom.co.za • www.hayhouse.co.za

Published in India by: Hay House Publishers India, Muskaan Complex, Plot No. 3, B-2, Vasant Kunj, New Delhi 110 070 • *Phone:* 91-11-4176-1620 • *Fax:* 91-11-4176-1630 • www.hayhouse.co.in

Distributed in Canada by: Raincoast, 9050 Shaughnessy St., Vancouver, B.C. V6P 6E5 • *Phone:* (604) 323-7100 *Fax:* (604) 323-2600 • www.raincoast.com